PRAISE FOR
relatable

"Rachel is so . . . relatable! This book feels like sitting down with your best friend or sister. She tells you like it is, but with love and compassion, and creates a blueprint for making connections and building relationships in a way that leaves you inspired and ready to take action."

–Andrea Owen, author of *Make Some Noise* and *How to Stop Feeling Like Shit*

"Whether she's talking on stage, TV, or TikTok, everything Rachel says is relatable. This book is packed with practical advice to help readers build better relationships with other people and with themselves. I highly recommend it!"

–Jessica Abo, author of *Unfiltered: How to Be as Happy as You Look on Social Media*

"In a world where we are always connected to devices, it's easy to lose what it truly means to connect to others. Rachel will help you release fears and any social anxiety so you can be your authentic self and create relationships that uplift every aspect of your life."

–Jessica Ornter, *New York Times* bestselling author and creator of the Tapping Solution app

"Rachel is part coach, part best friend, and the only plus one you'll need to walk you through your new more successful and more social life. Ultra-readable and full of hilarious stories and practical advice, rela*table* is the perfect book to guide you through your post-pandemic life"

–Samantha Ettus, bestselling author, iHeart podcast cohost, and entrepreneur

"If you're ready to break out of your shell and find your tribe, read this book! With her trademark humor and vulnerability, Rachel breaks down the skills you need to build strong social bonds that last."

–Parvati Shallow, *Survivor* **winner and life coach**

"relat*able* is the perfect title for this literary gem. Rachel clearly outlines the steps to getting out of your own way and digging to the root of why some are short-circuiting their own relationship success. This is a manual for anyone who is serious about connecting with others in a productive way."

–Calvin Roberson, author and relationship expert for *Married at First Sight*

"Must-read on relationship-building. Real examples. Real stories. And really useful advice, tips, and action steps to build the people skills necessary for success in your career and in your life. Two huge likeable thumbs up for relat*able*!"

–Dave Kerpen, bestselling author of *The Art of People*

"Connecting with others–and I mean truly and genuinely connecting–is an innate desire we all share. It's also an absolute must for corporate success and personal fulfillment. It has never been easy but thanks to Rachel's insightful, practical, and wonderful book, it will be significantly easier. Read it. Live it. Love it."

–Ron Tite, author of *Think Do Say*

relatable

relatable

HOW *to* CONNECT
with ANYONE, ANYWHERE
(EVEN IF IT SCARES YOU)

RACHEL DEALTO

SIMON ELEMENT
NEW YORK LONDON TORONTO SYDNEY NEW DELHI

**SIMON
ELEMENT**

An Imprint of Simon & Schuster, Inc.
1230 Avenue of the Americas
New York, NY 10020

First Simon Element trade paperback edition September 2022

SIMON ELEMENT is a trademark of Simon & Schuster, Inc.

For information about special discounts for bulk purchases, please contact Simon & Schuster Special Sales at 1-866-506-1949 or business@simonandschuster.com.

The Simon & Schuster Speakers Bureau can bring authors to your live event. For more information or to book an event, contact the Simon & Schuster Speakers Bureau at 1-866-248-3049 or visit our website at www.simonspeakers.com.

Interior design by Jennifer Chung

Manufactured in the United States of America

1 3 5 7 9 10 8 6 4 2

Library of Congress Cataloging-in-Publication Data

Names: DeAlto, Rachel, author.
Title: Relatable : how to connect to anyone, anywhere (even if it scares you) / by Rachel DeAlto.
Description: New York : Tiller Press, [2021] | Includes bibliographical references. | Identifiers: LCCN 2021011763 (print) | LCCN 2021011764 (ebook) | ISBN 9781982171087 (hardcover) | ISBN 9781982171094 (ebook) | Subjects: LCSH: Interpersonal relations. | Interpersonal communication. | Social phobia. | Social skills. Classification: LCC HM1106 .D424 2021 (print) | LCC HM1106 (ebook) | DDC 302-dc23
LC record available at https://lccn.loc.gov/2021011763
LC ebook record available at https://lccn.loc.gov/2021011764

ISBN 978-1-9821-7108-7
ISBN 978-1-9821-7110-0 (pbk)
ISBN 978-1-9821-7109-4 (ebook)

CONTENTS

Introduction   ix

PART ONE
The Why: Why relat*able*, Why Now?   1

    Chapter One: Far from Alone   2

    Chapter Two: Why People Like People   13

PART TWO
The How: Relate to Anyone, Anywhere   23

    Chapter Three: Connect–Authentically You   24

    Chapter Four: Connect–Confidence for Days   33

    Chapter Five: Connect–Power of Positivity   49

    Chapter Six: Communicate–Presence Over Presents   64

    Chapter Seven: Communicate–Flex Your Adaptability   75

    Chapter Eight: Communicate–Words Matter   85

    Chapter Nine: Inspire Your *Then What?*   95

PART THREE
The Who: How to Solve the Most Common People Problems   105

    Chapter Ten: Too Nice Isn't Sweet   106

    Chapter Eleven: It's Not You, It's Them   116

    Chapter Twelve: The Critical Smile   125

    Chapter Thirteen: Smizing Is Real   133

    Chapter Fourteen: The Last (Last) Word   143

Acknowledgments   147

Notes   148

relatable

INTRODUCTION

When I was eleven, while the other kids at school would play with their buddies on the playground, I was popping the heads off dandelions. By myself. I didn't have friends at school. Not a single one. Why? Well, I was an overweight know-it-all, my hand perpetually raised in the air, ready to answer every question posed by the teacher. Sadly, those calisthenics failed to result in my arm (or body) thinning out. By fifth grade, I was eating lunch with my teacher and avoiding recess altogether.

Then, the following year a miracle occurred: cue the arrival of Kaitlyn, the transfer student. She was clueless as to how ostracized I was at our school, and I was willfully ignorant of how odd she was. I didn't care. She was a potential friend, and that's all I needed to know.

Soon after meeting Kaitlyn and convincing her to like me, I was invited to her house for a sleepover. For a twelve-year-old loner, this was epic. I arrived promptly at 6 p.m. on her doorstep, accompanied by my Caboodle filled with ten shades of blue eye shadow to add to the sleepover fun. She answered her door, cradling her giant, hairy cat, Blueberry. My heart sank to my feet, yet I plastered a smile on my face. I refused to let her know I was *deathly* allergic to cats.

Unfortunately for me, Kaitlyn truly adored Blueberry and was insistent that I love him, too. Moments later, we were hanging out in her room, Warrant's "Cherry Pie" playing, and my eye shadows ready for application. Kaitlyn had other plans, though. Her cat and I must bond! As anyone allergic to animals knows, said furballs are always drawn to the person least able to give them affection.

Promptly, Blueberry jumped up into my lap, and by some miracle, I was still able to breathe–a win for the moment! Yet our cuddling was not enough. Blueberry thought it necessary to increase our connection, proceeding to mercilessly lick. my. face. I said nothing to Kaitlyn or my new paramour, believing my willpower would defeat my biology.

It turns out that biology is challenging to overcome. Within ten minutes, the hives pulsating on my face gave me the look of a Swamp Thing. Within eleven minutes, my parents were called, and I was whisked away, defeated, devastated, and headed for a heavy dose of Benadryl and a shower.

I'd been *so* desperate for connection that I was willing to endure dire illness to forge a friendship. A friendship that failed to launch after that fateful night, leaving me alone, and lonely, once again.

But I'm hardly alone. We *all* have an innate desire to belong. To connect. It's in our DNA to be social. Covid-19 has very clearly shown us that connection will always be essential. Various preventative measures have made many realize the value of human connection, as we scrambled to try to replicate in-person interactions—from happy hours to dates to meetings to conferences—with a virtual replacement. We adapted because the alternative of isolation felt unnatural and awful. We found a way to connect because it matters *that* much.

But that doesn't mean forming and maintaining connections is always easy.

Sometimes it's scary to start and sustain conversations with strangers, virtually and in person.

Sometimes it's scary to have those conversations with people we know.

Sometimes it's hard to know the right thing to say and how to say it.

Sometimes it's scary to be ourselves and vulnerable.

Sometimes it feels easier to avoid *all of it* altogether.

At any point, our social anxiety, fears, and trepidation can keep us from missing out on a fundamental component of the human experience: connection.

How often have you avoided an event because you were worried about feeling awkward? How many times have you dreaded going to a meeting or conference or date because you were afraid that they could smell how uncomfortable you felt? How often are you comfortable with being yourself? We've all been there. We've all had those moments where our hearts are beating so loudly that we swear the other person can hear it. Where we're not sure what to say, how to be, or why we chose to torture ourselves like this.

It's going to get easier, I promise, because helping people connect is my jam. It's what I've spent the last ten years doing and hopefully, for many more decades to come (especially if red wine is a preservative). It's a bit ironic that the trajectory of my current career began when I was a lawyer. "Lawyer" and "connector" aren't often two words you see together, but there I was, a litigator with a penchant for mediation and resolution. After I left the law to start a dating company (more on that later), it became second nature to help people navigate those treacherous waters as a coach. I began making media appearances where I could virtually support viewers in their dating lives and relationships on local New York City television stations. Those eventually led to regular appearances on shows like *Access Hollywood*, *Good Morning America*, *Steve Harvey*, and *Today*. All these appearances then culminated in my role as a relationship expert on *Married at First Sight* (*MAFS*, seasons four and five if you're looking for a Netflix binge) and *Kate+Date* on TLC, wherein I was able to exponentially increase the number of those I am able to reach with my advice and experience.

Of note, *MAFS* fans inspired the title of this book and my life's focus on relatability. After leaving the show, I received thousands of emails, DMs, and tweets from viewers upset about my departure. These messages were sweet, and I appreciated them very much, but there was also a common theme. A large majority of the messages cited my "relatability" as something they couldn't imagine easily replicated in a new expert. That made me think about what that truly meant, to be rela*table*. What was the audience seeing in me that made them feel connected? The resulting reflection, a subsequent master's in psychology, and working with clients has resulted in a blueprint for relatability that's been successful for so many from the boardroom to the bedroom.

I've created a method in rela*table* that works. These methods are what I've used with my individual clients and the organizations I've worked with. They've been tested in social and professional settings. They are going to help you take the steps needed to release all anxiety and start engaging.

rela*table* provides a road map to return us to what we are hardwired to do: relate and connect. Let's live authentically, get confident, become magnetic, and get out there and form meaningful relationships *right away*. There is no time like the present.

rela*table* is broken up into three parts:

1. The Why—You learn you are far from alone.
2. The How—Real tools, real stories, real ways to start becoming more relatable.
3. The Who—Particular people problems and how to solve them.

Introduction

Each chapter is meant to guide you through the process of becoming relatable with a mix of stories drawn from actual client experiences, stats, and pragmatic advice. I hope it's funny, but either way I laughed at my own jokes, so there's that. The pragmatic advice also includes steps to take to implement each chapter's lesson, an "Action" and a "Mindset."

The Action could be a reflection of past or present scenarios or actual actions I'd love for you to take. The purpose of the Action is in most cases to get you reflecting on the topics, how they apply to you, and what shifts you can make. Consider it a mini-journal, because journaling is awesome, therapeutic, and transformative, even in mini-form.

The Mindset is designed to give you a mantra. Yeah, I'm going all hippie on you. Our minds are extremely powerful, and I have seen time and time again where a shift in perspective changes everything. Trust me. It's meant to remind you in an "I am" statement (the most powerful kind of statement) that you are the embodiment of what that chapter discussed, that is, I am enough, I am open to new connections, I am a badass. Okay, the last one isn't actually in here, but it's true! It's okay if you don't believe every Mindset at first, but if you repeat it to yourself throughout the day it starts to stick.

Regardless of your starting point, you are on your way to improving the way you approach relationships, and kudos to you for taking this journey! I promise it will be worth it.

PART ONE

The Why: Why relatable, Why Now?

Chapter One

FAR FROM ALONE

VAUGHN

Vaughn walked into the cocktail party in a mood somewhere between completely content and excited. His boss had loved his ideas for the launch, it was payday, and he even made it to the gym twice that week. He knew this party was a necessary evil and that showing his face and appearing supportive to the client were essential, but he hadn't spent time overthinking it. Vaughn also knew that his boss would be in attendance and gregarious as always, so he wasn't overly concerned walking in. That is, until his phone buzzed in the pocket of his sport coat.

"Tied up at office. You're on. Don't disappoint me," wrote his boss. His first real boss. At his first real job. At his first cocktail party. For his first client.

Vaughn felt his heart starting to beat as if he had pressed the wrong button on the StairMaster, and like that dreadful machine, he knew this party was going to end up being much harder than it looked. Vaughn spotted the client, a tall, former pro football player known for a no-nonsense approach to everything and a bullshit sensor that worked from a mile away. Vaughn adjusted his tie, tried to muster up every ounce of courage he had, and began to walk in the client's direction through a sea of people who clearly had it together—at least far more than he did.

With each step, new beads of perspiration arose on Vaughn's forehead despite the subzero temperatures outside. His heart was now beating at a decibel that drowned out both the music and conversation surrounding him. As he landed in an appropriate radius to the client, Vaughn reached out his hand to introduce himself. Instead of responding in kind, the client bellowed an excited, "I'm so glad you could make it!" . . . to a man at the left of Vaughn's shoulder and began an engaging conversation.

Red-faced, shut out, and already quite sweaty, Vaughn retreated to the bar and to his iPhone. *I can't do this*, he thought as he sat alone. So, he didn't. After a while, Vaughn snuck out of the event without meeting the client, much to the disappointment of his boss—and himself.

Vaughn hadn't always been this anxious in social settings, and in his estimation, it was getting worse. In fact, among members of his generation—Millennials, commonly defined as the generation born between 1981 and 1996—general anxiety was collectively going from bad to worse.

Humans (yes, including Millennials) are wired for connection. We're wired to be social. As humans, we have ginormous brains—the largest in the animal kingdom proportionate to our size. Anthropologists tell us these giant noggins are built for socialization. Yet, in the last fifty years, we've become increasingly individualistic and less social despite the prevalence of the four billion people connected through social media.[1]

We've become the most disconnected society in recorded history at a time when we're the most connected by technology.

Technology is amazing, isn't it? We can stay connected to the world without leaving the comfort of the couch. We can order a three-course meal, watch seven seasons of a show (which should have been canceled after two), and search for our Prince(ss) Charming with a swipe of a thumb, all on our phones.

We don't even use doorbells anymore—unless it's to record video of every person who comes within fifty feet of our property. No one just "stops by" anymore; now we text "wya?"

A number of these changes are amazing improvements. Boundaries are awesome. Privacy is a phenomenal gift. If you show up on my doorstep on a Saturday morning at nine, I'm not answering. That's not all I won't answer. I believe there are two types of people in this world: those who answer incoming calls and those who stare at the screen, incredulous that someone had the audacity to hit send on anything other than a text message. One day, useless meetings will die too. #canthisbeanemail?

But what about our relationships? Are they surviving in a climate where we encourage everything to be conducted at arm's length and in acronyms?

It turns out they aren't.

People are socially anxious:

- **70 percent of people between the ages of eighteen and twenty-nine experience social anxiety, more than any other age group.**[2]
- **65 percent of Millennials avoid face-to-face conversations because they aren't confident in their abilities to interact.**[3]
- **30 percent of Millennials won't even attend events because they're afraid it's going to be socially uncomfortable.**[4]

As if all of this anxiety weren't enough, we're really freaking lonely, too, and the two are quite intertwined. In fact, we've never been lonelier.

A 2019 Cigna study that used the UCLA Loneliness Scale, a frequently cited and statistically proven assessment for loneliness levels, found that 45 percent of Millennials and 48 percent of Gen Zers were lonely.[5] Twenty-two percent of Millennials have no friends.[6] Not a single peer with whom to share the highs and lows of being human.

We can't survive on one meaningful interaction per week. Loneliness is dangerous. An often-cited 2015 Brigham Young study found that those without strong relationships had a risk of death equal to smoking fifteen cigarettes a day and double the risk of obesity.[7] Another study in the United Kingdom of almost 500,000 people over seven years found that "social isolation, similarly to other risk factors such as depression, can be regarded as a risk factor for poor prognosis of individuals with cardiovascular disease."[8] Heartache from loneliness is real. Your ticker may be fine at the moment, but it's extremely concerning if this trend continues.

Why, though? Why is this all happening now?

FOMO AND THE COMPARISON TRAP

Social media is an easy and typical scapegoat, though the data doesn't support blaming everything on social media. Even if social media use is not the cause of our loneliness, the comparison trap is real. In addition to our penchant for socialization, we are also natural comparers. In 1954, psychologist Leon Festinger first proposed social comparison theory, long before the internet was even a dream. Festinger hypothesized that we compare ourselves to and judge others as a way of self-evaluation, and that the impulse dates back to our innate need to protect ourselves—so basically forever.

The thing is, our cave people ancestors didn't have Instagram.

It's a different world from when I was in my twenties. I didn't have to walk five miles uphill in the snow to go to school, but I also didn't have to stare at pictures of my friends being offered amazing jobs while I struggled to make ends meet. I didn't have to see visual proof of my exes moving on with someone hotter than me, even when I unfriended every connection to them. I never had to see a video that showed me when I was left out of an event or party. We didn't know what we weren't invited to unless someone told us, and we never knew how fake-fabulous everyone's lives were.

Unless you live in a bubble, you can't help but compare yourself to the people that you see around you—it's science! Some comparisons can be healthy, inspirational even. If you see someone working out and looking fit, you may be inspired to work out yourself. If you see a friend traveling to Greece and posting amazing pictures, you may think, *Wow, I should travel more and stop working 100 percent of the time.*

On the flip side, it can also make us feel inadequate, especially if your self-esteem bucket is already less than full. Many compare from a negative viewpoint and feel surrounded by reminders that they're not doing enough, don't have enough, and aren't good enough.

This spiraling depletion of self-worth leads to isolation, fear, and anxiety. It's understandable that someone would want to avoid networking when everyone is seemingly more successful. It's understandable that someone would want to avoid conversations when everyone seemingly has it all together. But then, it's understandable that someone has trouble dating because they've seen every aspect of their competition's seemingly fabulous life.

It's understandable that we've become so anxious.

QUALITY OVER QUANTITY

Just text me!

I'll email you!

DM me!

If we think that our online conversations can replace face-to-face connections, we're going to become a very lonely society. Uh, wait a second . . . (scratches head).

It's pretty cool that we can do so much with just our thumbs, but while we may believe that our online interactions are just as good as connecting face-to-face, our brain does not agree. Research shows that people are happier after a face-to-face conversation versus an online interaction, and in-person time with family and friends can improve your quality of life versus virtual interactions.[9] It also changes how we connect, as another study found that when you compare in-person to virtual conversations among strangers, those who met face-to-face formed more positive impressions.[10] Perhaps the internet trolls need to meet the people they harass.

I know I feel it! I love the convenience of staying in touch with my friends and family on social. I know who got married, who had a baby, who got a dog. I see friends after years of not talking and feel like we're all caught up! Yet, I know the feeling I have when I spend real time with the humans I care about, and it's a hell of a lot different than when I commented on their picture. It's deeper, fuller, and much more heartwarming.

We're still connecting and staying in touch by messaging, commenting, liking, and sharing, but it's not deep enough to fulfill our biological needs of community.

Online communication and social media are great stepping-stones but not replacements. They are a side dish of delicious Brussels sprouts (don't judge) to a main course. Interacting solely or mostly online was not meant to be the norm. Think about it: If we limit all of our interactions to social media, emails, and texting, the world's population is in trouble!

We've created a me-versus-we society.

Our screens are not heart-filling.

Our communities are dwindling.

Our soul is suffering.

So, what do we do about it? Are we doomed?

Not a chance.

Let's get back to Vaughn. . . .

Vaughn is a smart, attractive, and awkward (in that adorable way) guy in his early twenties. He grew up in a tight-knit community where he had built-in friends on every surrounding block and was never alone. Think bike rides to his friends' houses every weekend, joint family barbecues, movie nights with his buddies, and a tab at the local pizzeria.

Vaughn's neighborhood and life were the epitome of optimal socialization. That is, until Vaughn's dad got a new job . . . two states away . . . right before he started high school.

Despite his parents' outgoing nature, life just wasn't the same after the move. While their family was friendly with their neighbors, there wasn't a sense of community in their new, sprawling suburban neighborhood. While their home and lot size tripled, their social network declined in a corresponding ratio. It's hard to re-create a lifetime of connections in months, especially when you had to drive to your next-door neighbor's house.

As Vaughn walked through the hallways as a freshman at a new high school, he found himself in the most unfamiliar of territories. There was no one to playfully bump into, no one to complain about history class with, and no one to make him feel like he belonged. So he dove into his phone, retreated inward, and while he focused on staying connected to his old friends, he had never felt so alone. It didn't help that in staying connected to his old life, Vaughn was reminded of what everyone else was doing . . . without him.

Vaughn felt that his phone and social media provided all the socialization he actually needed to survive high school. He met a few IRL friends during his teenage years but never really became involved in this new community. The quality of the relationships was nowhere near the ones he'd had in his old neighborhood.

Vaughn did fine in high school, but mostly, he was looking to get out and move on. He was lonely but not despondent. He had his Snapchat buddies. He could pass time watching endless YouTube videos, and he could play video games. He'd live.

Vaughn went on to college, where life was much the same. While he considered joining a fraternity, he ultimately decided that the rush process was overwhelming. Instead, he kept his head down, relying again on social media for connection, and plugged along until graduation.

He did well in school and graduated with honors. Yet in all the years following that fateful move (his dad is aware he's responsible for therapy), the only people that he would actually talk to were members of his family. He had grown apart from friends that he grew up with, and he found it easier to be alone than to put himself out there and make new ones.

He lived in New York City, and despite being surrounded by over eight million people, his loneliness was becoming overwhelming. While in school his "next" would keep him somewhat occupied–there was always something next to focus on, be it a paper, exam, event, or interview. When he landed his first job, for the first time there was no end in sight. There was just life.

Vaughn looked around and realized he was living this life completely by himself, and it was overwhelming.

What was more jarring was how anxious he felt about trying to change that feeling. He downloaded a dating app and swiped but never knew exactly what to say to start the conversation. His employer hosted networking events, but you already know what happened at his first one.

Vaughn contacted me not long after that dreadful night. His initial message was quite the SOS: "I'm not sure if you're the right person to help me, but I think I need help." We jumped on a quick phone call so I could assess the situation.

"So, sometimes I have trouble talking to people," Vaughn started.

"Sometimes?" I replied.

"Okay, most times," he admitted.

Vaughn tried to position himself as a guy who simply needed a quick fix.

"I probably only need one or two sessions so you can tell me what to do."

We met for coffee the following week to assess the situation. Vaughn's the kind of guy that you'd look at and never believe he had any "real problems." He's taller than average, has a decent build, and, though he's a bit nerdy, it's in a cute way. I would never pick him out of a lineup as the guy with social anxiety, but as he sat down in front of his venti half-caf, double cupped, salted caramel mocha latte, his face turned crimson.

"So. Uh. Yeah," he stammered.

He needed only one session like I need only one hour of sleep a night.

Vaughn suffered from what I would call "screen bravado." As long as he was behind a screen typing or talking, he could muster up his confidence at least enough to have a conversation. It became evident that Vaughn was actually very empathetic. When he became awkward in a face-to-face situation, he could feel the other person recognize his awkwardness and became uncomfortable as a result. All it did was reinforce his fear of having more of those in-person conversations. He was fully capable of talking, but it took a minute to warm up. And if the other person wasn't patient enough, that convo would go down in flames. Thankfully, my lack of patience is reserved for my children, so I was eventually able to get Vaughn to open up and feel more comfortable talking to me.

I asked how it was for him at work. He explained, "It was rough at first. I was hired virtually during my senior year in college. My interviews were over Skype, so they couldn't see my hands shaking. During my first week I could tell my boss was wondering if he'd made a mistake hiring me."

The saving grace was that Vaughn was good at his job. Really good. He had creative ideas and no problem sharing them–over email. His boss chalked up Vaughn's lack of engagement at the water cooler to his age and relative newness.

But Vaughn knew that his advancement would be significantly hindered if he didn't resolve his apprehension around social exchanges. And the loneliness he felt on his couch on a Friday night would only intensify.

In the beginning, I would ghostwrite his text messages and emails for him verbatim, because even though he was more comfortable behind a screen, he wanted to make sure he wouldn't turn off a potential date, aggravate his boss, or repel a potential friend. If he had a networking event (which was a requirement of our working together) or was meeting someone new, we would prepare all week. I'd walk him through each step and check in throughout the night. It was awkward and uncomfortable at first, but with practice, he started to shift. Social skills and confidence increase just like our muscles do with workouts, so that the more you work out, the more conditioned you become. The heavier you lift, the larger your muscles grow. Eventually, Vaughn outgrew me, and I couldn't have been prouder.

I've since met a lot of Vaughns. So many people who have isolated themselves socially because of anxiety or the cycle of loneliness, or both, now arriving at the conclusion that life may be a whole lot better if you had deeper connections. Yet, there is always a level of fear.

It's understandable. Networking at a business event can feel like you're being picked for a dodgeball team all over again. I teach connection for a living, and there are times when I walk into an event knowing no one, and even I become tempted to hide in a corner, avoid eye contact, and play on my phone while slowly eating the crudités I don't even like that much. It's a lot easier to live behind a screen where you can connect with people at a distance. There's no risk of face-to-face rejection, and you can perfect your replies before hitting send, comment, or submit.

We have to push ourselves even if it's uncomfortable. We don't get better by avoiding the situations that make us feel awkward. If we avoid events and/or people, we feed the beast and reinforce the fear. The more fear we feed, the harder that first step becomes.

When I was three years old, I was bitten in the face by a spider. Half of my face swelled beyond recognition while the other remained completely normal, like one of those makeup demonstrations gone wrong. My parents rushed me to the ER, fearing that I was in anaphylactic shock. The doctors gave me a shot of an antihistamine and the swelling subsided. I recovered, but from that point on I was completely and utterly an arachnophobe.

Throughout my life, my screams would alert my parents that there was another spider to kill in my presence. It didn't matter how big, small, or harmless, the shriek was the same decibel. There was always someone to save me, until my sophomore year of college, when I found myself renting an apartment solo (told you I like my privacy). My landlord was very confused as to why there were dents in the ceiling created by a girl who couldn't reach it. Did you know that phone books are really efficient at killing those eight-legged terrifiers and they're throwable? It's really a shame that the internet killed the use of said books. So useful.

For more than twenty years, I lived with this terror, until I considered getting treated for my fear. "Exposure therapy" was suggested. Come again? You'd like me to cuddle a tarantula? I'd rather light myself on fire, thank you very much.

Interestingly, for someone with a fear of spiders (and frankly not a fan of other bugs), I decided to host a retreat in the jungles of Mexico. There weren't even walls. We slept in *palapas* and were one with nature for seven days straight. I doused myself in bug spray and created a fortress of peppermint oil around my bed, but *my God* the bugs and spiders I lived among. They were everywhere—some the size of my head, and my head is big.

I could have freaked out, but I was responsible for twenty people who were also having a hard time welcoming their new insect friends. I made it through without being eaten alive and arrived home not even realizing the transformation—until I saw my first post-Mexico spider. Now, listen, I didn't hug it, but I also didn't lose my mind. I proved unknowingly and unintentionally that exposure therapy works.

Why am I sharing a story about me being a complete wuss? Because exposure therapy may work for you, too. Putting yourself in those uncomfortable situations can help to lessen anxiety around those interactions. Don't worry, I'm not going to throw you in the jungle and make you sleep without walls. (Seriously, what was I thinking?) But I will help you to look that fear in the eye and overcome it without bug spray. In fact, every chapter in this book will provide you with a game plan for surviving those exposures.

What happens when you step out of your comfort zone? You make magic.

The anxiety and loneliness felt in this world is holding us back. Our success will hit a glass ceiling. Our happiness will be compromised.

Our relatability can resolve these challenges.

Growing comfortable in your own skin, building connections, and creating real relationships will change everything, from the way you feel to the level of your success in your career.

As a speaker, I often see companies hiring Millennial or Gen Z speakers to teach the older staff how to collaborate with a young workforce. But who is helping *you* overcome the situation we've created? I find it coincidental that the computer geeks who invented the internet, Vinton Cerf and Bob Kahn (not Al Gore, sorry), are part of the Silent Generation, born in 1938 and 1943, respectively. While the silence of that generation was due to the Great Depression and a world war, the silence today is largely influenced by their creation. We don't talk to one another. We don't connect. But we can change that.

It all starts now.

LET'S DO THIS!

ACTION:

Do you feel anxious in social settings? If so, why do you believe you feel that way?

_____

_____

_____

Describe your ideal self in a social environment. How do you feel, what are you doing, who are you talking to? Write it as if you are there in the moment.

_____

_____

_____

What steps can you take (even before getting to Chapter Two!) to improve your relationships?

_____

_____

_____

MINDSET: I am open to new connections.

Chapter Two

WHY PEOPLE LIKE PEOPLE

MELANIE

I believe we all have a Melanie in our lives.

My Melanie simply sparkled. Though we were all required to wear a uniform to the private high school we attended, Melanie's uniform was always a bit crisper. While the rest of us mortal teen girls were dealing with the onslaught of clogged pores and disobedient hair, her pearly skin was flawless and her blond mane, gleaming. When she turned seventeen, she pulled her brand-new pearly white BMW 3 Series up next to my clunker hand-me-down 1988 Crown Victoria. It had more than 150,000 miles on it, a black door on a gray body, and an engine that liked to stall in the rain. While Melanie was riding in style, thanks to her parents, I sold my car to a man named Alone (his real name, I swear on my dog's happiness) for a hundred dollars after it had died for the hundredth time. True story.

I envied Melanie. We all did. Melanie had a seemingly perfect life that made her the It Girl in school. She was the one everyone clambered to sit with at lunch. The one every guy wanted to take to prom. The one that we all knew would go on to marry the perfect guy, give birth to the perfect kids, and continue to live her perfect life in cars that would never die on the freeway. There was no doubt about it.

Flash forward to ten years after high school. I was sitting in the local Starbucks, shopping online, but pretending to work, when my retail therapy was interrupted by a "Rachel?"

I looked up, furrowed my forehead (pre-Botox, these things were possible), and I stammered, "Melanie?" In truth, I was unsure. She resembled the Melanie I remembered, but the woman before me was the physical incarnation of how you would feel after a bottle of rosé, two hours of sleep, and arriving like a tornado an hour late to an important meeting.

She plopped down in the chair across from me, panting, and replied, "Yep. It's me. It's been a while, hasn't it?"

Uh, yeah, Melanie, what the hell happened to you?

I swear I only asked that question in my head, but my curiosity must have flashed across my face, because she went on to say, "It's been a rough decade. My parents split after my dad got arrested for insider trading. They're now broke and hate each other. Actually, they always hated each other, but my mom loved the money."

She continued, "I dropped out of college when we couldn't afford the tuition and moved in with my mom. Everyone has cut me off. No one is interested in spending time with the daughter of a felon whose BMW got repossessed."

Woah. I was not prepared for that. First of all, those were more words than we had ever exchanged in high school. I never really knew Melanie. I knew the image she portrayed. I knew what everything seemed to be. I never knew that beneath the apparent perfection, there was the pain of parents who detested each other, the disproportionate value placed on wealth, and a lack of real friendships.

All of a sudden, I wanted to find my beater Crown Vic and hug it. I'm sure Alone wouldn't mind the company.

If you would have told my high school self that Melanie would have any of this happen to her, I'd have flipped my hair and proclaimed in my best Cher Horowitz, "as if." Yet here she was with the entire foundation of her life crumbled. No longer sparkly, rich, or popular, she felt she was at the bottom and completely on her own. Her friends were never real friends, but acquaintances. Her relationships had no depth. In the months leading up to her father's arrest, she was one of the most popular in her sorority at college. Yet when the shit hit the proverbial fan, she was left to pick up the pieces without a support system. All that glitters is not gold. Sometimes, it's just gold coated.

In high school, we avoided scratching below the surface, putting our faith in superficial traits like so many high school kids do. Like in every teenage Netflix series, we honor the pretty people. The athletes. The rich kids. Most learn with age and personality maturity that we are far more than our reflections, bank accounts, and body fat percentages.

Thankfully, high school is not real life. Or is it?

WE'RE DOING IT ALL WRONG

Turns out, we still think an image of perfection is necessary to make people like us, love us, and work with us. We place a disproportionate amount of emphasis on superficial qualities. We filter ourselves until we're unrecognizable on social media. We post only the highlights of our lives. We hide the parts of ourselves that we think wouldn't be accepted.

We lie. A lot.

Did you know that 60 percent of adults lie at least once in a ten-minute conversation?[1] Our online lives are one big worldwide web of lies, and sadly, we expect it! Only 32 percent maintain they are always honest on social media, and a measly 2 percent expect honesty.[2]

We even lie in therapy. In a 2016 study, researchers found a whopping 93 percent had lied consciously at least once to their therapist.[3] Fifty-four percent minimized their psychological distress and pretended to be happier and healthier than they actually were. C'mon now! In the very place where our vulnerability can help us, we are projecting a "better" version of ourselves.

What is the impact of our lies on our relationships? On us? How can we truly connect with someone while lying . . . or being lied to? We can't.

Our lies are killing real relationships, stressing us out, and are terrible for our health.[4]

The irony of all of our fibbing is that while we are trying to make people like us, we are missing out on the key ingredient—honesty. In a 2015 study at the University of California, Los Angeles, participants rated adjectives in terms of their "perceived significance to likeability."[5] Authenticity, sincerity, and capacity for understanding ranked the highest.

Authenticity. Being authentic. Genuine. Real.

Sincerity. Honest. Lacking deceit. Free from pretense.

Capacity for understanding. Empathy. Compassion.

While we continue overfiltering to create an image of perfection, human beings are craving real people with emotional intelligence.

Yet large shallow networks feed your ego. Real authentic connections feed your soul.

A well-known Harvard study on adult development spanning nearly eighty years found that "close relationships, more than money or fame, are what keep people happy throughout their lives."[6]

Close relationships, not acquaintances, not followers, not likes. Close relationships keep us happy. Close relationships lead to opportunity and success.

So what do we do now?

Ready for some good news? You can learn how to be likeable and relat*able*. Becoming relat*able* combines likeability with relationship building–it means that you are able to relate to another and form connections. These are not inherent traits like blue eyes or black hair. If you were a five-foot-five college freshman with dreams of playing in the NBA, we would be discussing expectation management. Conversely, we have the opportunity to address abilities that can be molded, built, and mastered, regardless of where you are starting from.

My goal is that you begin to rethink every interaction, every connection, and every relationship.

How can you take the contents of this book and have a better experience in every interaction, online and IRL?

How can you use these tools to become confident in those interactions and reap the benefits they provide? Hello, lowered stress and happiness!

Professionally, I've been observing people for decades, first as a litigator and then as a relationship expert. As divergent as those paths may seem, they both center upon reading humans.

Those who ace relationship building do three things, and they do them *very* well:

They connect.

They communicate.

And they inspire.

Throughout relat*able*, we will dive deeper into each of these foundational principles as well as their nuances, but here is a glimpse of what's to come:

Connect. Chapters Three to Five. Your ability to connect is at its highest potential when you are authentically yourself, confident, and positive. We will remove the filters and set the stage so you can show up as yourself, beautiful imperfections and all. We will embrace our inner badass and learn to release negative self-talk. Life may not always be rainbows and unicorns, but we will learn to embrace positive thinking and choose optimism.

Communicate. Chapters Six to Eight. Unlike other books on communication, we will travel a different road, one where we focus on the emotional intelligence required to become a great communicator. One must feel seen and heard in order to feel connected. In an age where phubbing (phone snubbing) is now a thing, how can we become more present? We will also explore the art of adaptability, where using our "capacity for understanding" is essential, and we'll wrap up with the semantics of communication. Words matter.

Inspire. Chapter Nine. Excelling at connecting and communicating will leave you heads above the rest, but then what? Inspire to take things to the next level. It's time to identify your *then what?* We're going to make you a beacon of light that draws people in, like bugs to a zapper, only without the death and awful cleanup.

Chapters Ten to Twelve will also include how to handle the challenges you may face as you work to make these connections. People pleasers and the boundaryless: I'm looking at you.

Chapter Thirteen is your road map to remaining rela*table* in a world where we have more interactions via video than in person and our eyes are now not only the windows to our soul, but have to carry the expressions of our entire face while masked up.

rela*table* will provide the road map you need to:

- **Expand your social networks—platonically and romantically**
- **Create deeper relationships with existing connections**
- **Build sustainable and meaningful professional relationships**

You're already hardwired to do this. I'm only helping to pave the way and make the journey easier.

BE VERSION 2.0

Anyone can become rela*table*. Even if they were initially downright offensive. Even if they were quite literally called the Worst. Someone could become universally liked even after ruining the reputation of my birthplace.

I am lucky to live in a beautiful coastal region that spans 130 miles along the Atlantic Ocean. For thirty years, two months, and four days of my life, no one really knew much about my area of the shore, unless you lived or vacationed here. Most people I encountered in my travels solely associated New Jersey with Newark International Airport and its surrounding oil refineries. I had no desire to correct them, as we didn't need any additional tourists taking over our amazing beaches in the summer.

Then, after 11,023 days of beautiful anonymity, a little TV show started airing on MTV, and everything changed for us locals.

Jersey Shore.

The reality series followed the antics of eight very tan and heavily hair-sprayed housemates as they summered at the beach in New Jersey. The majority of their time was spent partying and fighting, and the show became a pop culture sensation almost immediately. Over a decade later, when someone asks me where I'm from, they respond with fist pumps and an "untz, untz, untz." (You just said that to yourself, didn't you?)

I could take the time to argue that only two of the eight initial cast members were from New Jersey. Snookie is from Poughkeepsie, New York, for Pete's sake. Or I could explain that my area of the shore is peaceful and tranquil, devoid of loud clubs and cars with the bass set so loud you feel your brain loosen from the stem, but that would be a tad petty.

Amid the cast that failed to accurately represent New Jerseyans (okay, okay, I'll stop) was an individual by the name of Michael Sorrentino, aka The Situation.

The Situation (also called Sitch for short) was given the moniker because his "abs are so ripped up, it's called 'the situation.'" He was loud, obnoxious, and heavily involved in the GTL (gym/tanning/laundry) lifestyle that the show made famous. His days were spent keeping his abs in check. His nights involved heavy partying, objectifying as many women as possible, and creating drama at every turn.

Mike was the poster child for superficial. While annoying and arrogant at the outset, he became increasingly less likeable and cockier as the seasons went on. A 2013 article named him one of "The Worst People in Reality TV History."[7]

Then he hit a wall. Quite literally.

While filming in Italy, Mike slammed his head into a concrete wall, thinking it was drywall. Ouch. He later admitted that the incident involved self-induced withdrawal to Percocet, as the prescription drug was not readily available overseas.

Following that incident, Mike sought treatment for substance abuse issues and after three rounds in rehab, became sober in 2015. In addition to his addictions, Mike was also charged with tax fraud and eventually served an eight-month sentence in federal prison. It was quite the fall from toned and tanned grace.

In 2018, the cast was reunited for *Jersey Shore: Family Vacation*. Mike showed up nearly unrecognizable. He was kind, respectful, self-aware, and sober. He humbled himself. Completely. He took responsibility for his actions, was honest about his faults, and built solid relationships with his cast members and his now wife.

The Situation, who was very entertaining but holy unlikeable, became . . . endearing. He was real and oh-so-relatable. Even if you don't relate to him personally and haven't shared similar experiences, you were able to witness his humanity and feel connected to him. A fete for reality television, and I should know!

I'd have no desire to sit down and have a coffee with the OG Situation, but Mike 2.0? Absolutely.

The road to becoming more likeable and relat*able* can be bumpy and winding. I've been there myself, and I'm thankful that my road back didn't involve rehab or cranial injuries. In my grammar school years, I was eat-with-your-teacher friendless. There were no sleepovers, no playdates, no games at recess. It was just me, my brain, and thirty extra pounds. I would attribute my lack of popularity partly to my added weight amid a sea of J.Crew kid models (possibly RIP J.Crew), but the reality was that I was annoying.

I thought I knew everything, and I made that belief known with my perpetually raised hand and air of superiority as I answered every question correctly. I was loud (still am) and opinionated (yep, still that, too) but with little emotional intelligence to understand that my actions were a repellent. I still craved friends and relationships. I just didn't know how to make them at ten.

Thankfully, my emotional intelligence grew as I did. I began to recognize that if I shifted the way I acted, even slightly, I could be smart *and* likeable. I used my ears as much as my mouth. I learned the power of self-deprecating humor. I saw that confidence isn't a bad thing, but arrogance is going to push most people away.

In the end, we are simple creatures. The more real you are, the deeper your relationships can be. We are drawn to people who make us feel good, people who listen and engage, those who are honest and authentic, and those who make us feel better than before.

"I've learned that people will forget what you said, people will forget what you did, but people will never forget how you made them feel."
–Maya Angelou

The chapters that follow will help you be that person. You're one step closer to becoming irresistibly likeable.

LET'S DO THIS!

ACTION:

Make a list of the most likeable people in your life and their traits.

_____

_____

_____

Where do you believe you have room for growth to become more likeable?

_____

_____

_____

MINDSET: I am likeable and easy to connect with.

PART
TWO

The How: Relate to Anyone, Anywhere

Chapter Three

CONNECT—
AUTHENTICALLY
YOU

Take a moment to think about the last person you met and felt an instant connection with. Someone about whom you thought, *I would love to spend more time with this person,* or *That person could totally be my friend,* or *Wow, I would love to work with them.* It doesn't happen all that often, but when it does, it's undeniable.

What was it about this person that made you think these thoughts? I guarantee it wasn't because they led with the type of car they drive, how expensive their shoes were, or how incredibly brilliant their last idea was. It's never the person more consumed with their reflection than the conversation. It's deeper than that.

The people we instantly feel connected to feel *real.*

True connection happens when we are being ourselves. A bond forms in the moment you drop the act, mask, and facade of perfection to reveal your genuine self. We have to be willing to reveal our authentic selves in order to allow people to truly relate to us. Yet, in spite of this, we often put on a variety of masks because we think that the people whom we meet will only want to connect with us, like us, love us, join our organization, or hire us if we're perfect. Turns out, perfection is a lie. No one is perfect. No one can attain perfection. And no one expects it of you. Still here we are, believing that it's a requirement.

A study of more than 40,000 college students found that between 1989 and 2016, perfectionism increased 10 percent in terms of one's internal belief that they should be perfect, that is, "I expect myself to be perfect."[1] The more startling stat was the 33 percent increase due to social pressures to be perfect, that is, "Others expect me to be perfect."[2] I guess it shouldn't be that big a surprise, though, considering the corresponding invention and rise of social media.

Nearly four billion people use social media throughout the world, and the number is expected to continue to grow. Social media creates an opportunity to expand our networks far beyond what was possible twenty years ago, but are the connections being made genuine and lasting? When a person can be Photoshopped, Facetuned, and filtered beyond recognition? When someone can pretend to share their life through posts and stories, but the truth is those positive moments are few and far between?

It's a different world compared to twenty years ago. The pressure to be perfect existed, but it was far more a microcosm than the environment we are in now. Our families, friends, and classmates or colleagues were the source of our "never quite perfect" angst. Sure, I had plenty of schoolyard bullies to keep me in check, er, traumatized, but I made it through college unscathed by the comments of random strangers on the interweb. I never had to learn that @bob12974 thought my eyebrows were crooked until I was thirty. I recognize that many readers did not have that luxury and will not, that kids in grammar school have Instagram profiles and TikTok accounts, that your life has been on display since day one because we have become a social media society. It's impossible to talk about authenticity without recognizing how impacted we are by this medium that creates impossibly perfect imagery.

CHECK YOUR FILTERS

A short time ago, I attended an event filled with "influencers." Some of the women I had been following for quite some time; I admired their posts, wanted to buy the clothes they repped, and thought we would totally get along over a cocktail. Yet here we were face-to-face, with free cocktails pouring, and I didn't. even. recognize. them. I'm not talking about taking a moment to reconcile a still image online versus a real live person, I'm saying they looked *completely* different. Even more jarring, they acted completely differently. They were completely different people! It was bananas. These people had created a persona that *only* lived online. One that may translate into likes and comments but fails to create relationships of substance.

How could they when they are nowhere near the same person in real life?! They aren't alone! Turns out we all lie online, *and* we expect it from everyone else. A study found that only 16 to 32 percent are honest online, but 0 to 2 percent expected others to be honest![3] We are really taking the phrase "web of lies" to a whole new level.

It's not that the advent of filters is a terrible innovation; it's not. But like most innovations, we need to remember the lessons of Icarus. Icarus, the son of Daedalus in Greek mythology, was given a set of wings created by his father to allow him to fly and escape imprisonment by King Minos. Daedalus warned Icarus not to fly too close to the sun, because the wax attaching the wings would melt. Icarus, like my kids, ignored his parents, and flew too close to the sun anyway. His wings melted, and he fell into the sea and drowned. Dark, right? It's supposed to be, since it's a cautionary tale. Inventions can be fantastic, but we should be wary of overusing them, especially when the overuse of these tools masks who we really are.

Prior to Facetune and Photoshop, you'd hear men and women alike saying, "Take the picture from there. This is my good side." The difference is, we've stopped showing who we are, and we started showing who we wish we were. Don't forget, your "good side" is still a side of your true self.

It is far easier to filter than to accept who you are. It's far easier to pretend to be perfect online than to embrace being a work in progress. Know that you can want to transform yourself and still be authentically content with who you are in the moment. Fly high, filter away, just don't get too close to the sun. I advise everything in moderation–like my wine!

CHECK YOURSELF

It's not only our appearances we are filtering, it's our entire life. It's not just on social media; we lie in real life, too. In the last chapter we learned that lies run rampant in human conversations. Americans lie eleven times a week on average.[4] Lying isn't only bad for your health, it's terrible for your relationships.[5]

In every aspect of relationship building, authenticity is an essential element. Think about it: If no one knows who you truly are, how can they really connect with you? Whether we are selling ourselves (figuratively, of course) or something tangible, we must strive to be real.

I learned a tremendous amount about myself, and the human condition in general, when I became an attorney. Did you know that 28 percent of attorneys suffer from mild or higher levels of depression?[6] No one highlights that in law school brochures!

Prior to passing the bar, I was fortunate to enjoy a good degree of success throughout my law school journey. I did well in the classroom and was lucky to land a sought-after position as a summer associate at a prestigious firm. Summer associates could go on to be offered a full-time position after graduating from law school, and most partners begin on that track. I could taste my future success.

The firm was very no-nonsense and white glove. Employees worked hard, but I never saw them play hard. They kept a refreshment cart roaming the halls at all times to make sure we were perpetually caffeinated, and all attorneys were to be addressed as Mr. or Mrs. or Ms. The almighty billable hours were king and your commitment to the bottom line above everything else was required.

Each day I would arrive at 7:30 a.m. and half of the partners were already at their desks dictating away on their latest brief. Associates running "late" (that is, not arriving until 8:00 a.m.) would have a colleague pour a cup of steaming coffee and leave it on their desk so it still appeared that they were in the office.

In the evening, I would sneak out around 6:30 p.m., which was right around the time when most of the attorneys were getting their second wind. I'd "forget" to turn off my light just in case a partner walked by and took notice. Burning the midnight oil was not only a colloquialism at the firm but a way of life.

In addition to case files that covered the floors in all offices, the attorneys would spend their evenings at the requisite networking dinners and cocktail parties and turn right back around to spend their mornings at breakfast meetings. Their workload challenged even the most time-efficient human being, and yet they stayed the course. It was actually quite impressive.

As for myself, I did my work, and I did it well, but I know they questioned why I wasn't there with the other summer associates at 8 p.m. I know they questioned why I would take work home over the weekend rather than spend my Sunday in the office. I know they wondered why, at 9 p.m., I would slink out of the networking event when the wine was still freely flowing. I know they wondered why a twenty-four-year-old woman was apparently less committed than her counterparts. And I know with the utmost certainty that they had absolutely no idea what I was hiding. . . .

My four-year-old son.

Do you know how exhausting it is to hide a human being?

I avoided conversations that became too personal. I would smile and nod if someone spoke about their personal life, but I never contributed. It also became evident that I might not fit in. When one partner was asked, "So, how many kids do you have, Bob?" he replied, "Four, but don't ask me their names and ages, it'll make me look bad." Another associate joked that he had no idea who his child's teacher was. Ever. For the past nine years. I mean, I'm far from the PTA president, but even I could name most of my son's.

Have you ever wanted to fit in somewhere so badly that you tried to become a different person?

Clearly there was a deep-rooted culture at the firm. One that rewarded a lack of liabilities and a focus on the work. One that might not work for a single mom with a four-year-old.

I chose an industry that was cutthroat and competitive, and where my chance to be brought on full-time could be dependent on face time at the office. Where my chance to be a partner could be hindered by loving something or someone more than billable hours. And I had been judged heavily in the past for having a child so young. It was a perfect storm.

So, I hid. I hid the most amazing part of me, that I was a mom, and one who loved her child fiercely and would always choose him over work. I was undoubtedly afraid. I was afraid of being perceived as less than perfect. I was worried about being judged. I was worried about losing a lucrative opportunity.

What does lying or omitting the truth do to a budding relationship? It certainly doesn't help matters. It turns out that it's a bit difficult to hide a child forever. I eventually did tell everyone about my son, and they were shocked–after all, I had been at the firm for nearly two years at that point. They said they understood, and I was eventually (and in my opinion begrudgingly) offered that full-time position, which I declined in pursuit of a better fit for my family.

Even though this was simply not the appropriate environment for me, let's look at what that lie did: It broke trust. It shifted the way I was viewed. The image of perfection was shattered, not because of my son but because of my lie.

It's not the crime that damages things. It's the cover-up. We can't trust people who lie to us. We can't connect with those who aren't themselves.

I have no idea what would have happened if I had told the truth from the beginning. I will never know. All I am aware of is the anxiety of pretending to be someone I'm not. So I can tell you this for certain: It is *exhausting* to pretend to be perfect. There were two alternative possibilities–both freeing, for that matter. I could have been honest from the start, and with their acceptance, paved a new way within the firm where my responsibilities could be met without the expected face time. Or, I could have been honest, not been offered the position, and thereby recognize that this position was not ideal for me, my overall success, or my happiness.

We hide things from others because of our own perception. We create an internal narrative that prevents the sharing of our stories and lives, when with a different approach our past could be recognized as a strength. We're so afraid of rejection that we're inclined to pretend as if we've had a perfect life.

How many times have you been drawn to someone who pretended to be perfect? Frankly, most of the time I guarantee they annoy the crap out of you.

Sure, I had my son at a young age, but I also graduated with honors from college and then law school while being a mom. It wasn't easy, and I've had to cover some early grays, but it was worth every sleepless night. My path is one that people can relate to and identify with–my imperfections can create relatability. We all have pasts and challenges that we have overcome on our path to success. Maybe we don't talk about them. Maybe we should. If sharing who you are, what you've overcome, and what makes you *you* leads to rejection by anyone, then they are not your people.

Our stories shape who we are. Our stories help us connect.

But what about the fear that comes from sharing something so intimate?

I just shared a very personal story. It's vulnerable, and I'm aware that sharing a story that personal may not feel comfortable to some. However, from this moment on, I want to encourage us to start to share more of ourselves with everyone that we meet.

Do you notice that when you share something, people often feel the need to reciprocate and share in return? If we start sharing some of the authentic and vulnerable parts of ourselves, we can encourage others to do the same.

It can be hard to be vulnerable and authentic, to share your story the first time, to share your truth. I can guarantee, the moment you are accepted for being *you*, everything changes. What if our confidence levels are declining because of how we are showing up in the world?

Why do you feel the need to filter the truth?

ALLY

Ally came to me for help in her search for love. She was a beautiful forty-two-year-old woman, financially secure, and professionally accomplished. She had been divorced for nearly five years and was frustrated with the dating scene. Ally had been on hundreds of first dates over those five years but rarely had a second, and no date led to a relationship of any length.

We talked about her efforts to meet Mr. Right, and given her busy schedule, Ally focused on dating apps to meet most of her dates. I asked Ally to send me her dating profiles and read them with my mouth agape. Every picture was edited and filtered beyond recognition. Her description was of someone else entirely. She talked about loving camping when I knew that her idea of the great outdoors was an open-air shopping mall.

No wonder there were never second dates! Imagine if you show up for drinks, excited to meet this person you had been chatting with, only to discover that they looked completely different in real life. And those shared interests? They weren't real, either.

I asked Ally, "Why wouldn't you just be you? Why so many filters? Why not share your actual interests?"

She replied, "Because I'm not enough just as me."

Those feelings of "not enough," that lack of self-love, is often the reason why we are scared to show our true selves. It becomes a vicious cycle, and in cases like Ally's she perpetuated those feelings of "not enough" through the rejections of her dates. It begs the question, though: What if she had put herself out there—her real self? I guarantee that the lack of second dates was not because of her lack of attractiveness or overall appeal; I would surmise that it was because her dates felt duped. Not the best foundation to start any relationship.

We cannot heal what we can't see, and if you're afraid of being more authentic, it's time to shine a light on your why. Why is it really scary to let someone in? Why do you hide the truth? Fear of rejection, judgment, or feeling less than can be overcome with action.

It's time to start playing the role of yourself.

THE LAST WORD . . .

Be vulnerable. Tear off the mask and share your story. I don't have a burning desire to bare my soul to the world, but I know I have an obligation to let people know they aren't alone. I know that every time I share even parts of my story, I connect with someone new who can see their own journey from a different perspective. Share what has made you strong. Leaders and lovers alike require vulnerability to truly connect.

Large networks of shallow depth feed ego. Deep, authentic connections feed your soul.

LET'S DO THIS!

ACTION:

Think about a time when you were being inauthentic, intentionally or reflexively. Describe the way you presented yourself.

_____

_____

_____

What was the situation? How did the other person react?

_____

_____

_____

Describe how you wish you had acted.

_____

_____

_____

What stands in the way of you presenting yourself authentically? How can you overcome this?

_____

_____

_____

How can you commit to becoming more authentic in your interactions?

_____

_____

_____

MINDSET: I am enough.

Chapter Four

CONNECT— CONFIDENCE FOR DAYS

CHRIS

Chris walked into the meeting with a strain in his chest that he tried to push down like a French press. Unfortunately, rather than creating a delicious highly caffeinated beverage, his efforts led to anxiety spreading to the rest of his upper body. He knew the numbers were bad. He knew his department heads were as stressed as he was and looking for guidance or some sort of life raft. Overworked and underappreciated employees filled the company.

Clenching his jaw in a last-ditch effort to regain composure, Chris settled into the large leather seat at the head of the conference room, wondering if it would make him feel better to slam his fist and shatter the overpriced glass table.

"We have to do better," he began. "*You* have to do better. What the hell is wrong with your teams? Have you seen these numbers? They're disgraceful. This falls on you. Your numbers either improve by the end of the month, or you're done here." With that Chris stormed out of the meeting, attempting to slam the door behind him but failing due to the hydraulic hinge. *Awkward.*

As he retreated to his office, Chris heaved a sigh of relief. He had delivered the message. Yet the tightness remained. He put his team's jobs on the line, but he knew his own position remained unstable unless sales improved. He slumped down in his overpriced executive chair and muttered, "I suck at this."

Chris was very smart. Brilliant even. He could look at a situation and see where the holes were with an intuitive understanding of how to fix them. Data and Chris were soul mates. He was a mastermind when it came to business, which is why he was named his company's youngest CEO at forty-one.

Relationships, though? That was another story. Chris was divorced and uninterested in jumping in the dating pool ever again. He had a few friends but no one that he was truly close with. His nowhere-to-be-found social skills directly translated into poor leadership. He adopted the *Bronx Tale* method of leading, wherein he would rather be feared than loved–a method he'd employed since college.

Throughout his adolescence, Chris's intelligence never translated to popularity. In high school, he found himself with his head down, focused on work, and lonely. He was ambitious though, and so convinced himself that with a Ferrari and a penthouse, this emptiness would be eventually filled.

A studious creature, Chris began observing those he deemed successful around him: the bond trader he interned for, the father of his friend who ran a multimillion-dollar company, his mother's boss at the law firm. The problem was, they were all . . . well, assholes. It was then, as an impressionable sixteen-year-old with high ambition and a giant brain, that he decided to take a different approach in college and become . . . an asshole.

Chris adopted the "fake it till you make it" approach, and it worked. His fake arrogance landed him a circle of friends (or at least acquaintances he could pretend were friends) and women with equally low self-esteem whose only desire was to make him like them. His fabricated ego got him jobs, a wife (albeit only for a year), and success.

All the while, underneath it all, Chris was still a highly intelligent overachiever with no real self-esteem or social skills. He spent more than twenty years hiding behind a cocky pretense that may have worked when sales were high, but the pomposity that got him to his CEO position was not going to help him save a sinking ship.

Chris didn't want to work with me. A board member attended a keynote I had given on leadership at a conference and suggested bringing me in, not for Chris, but for the management teams. The day that I came in, I entered his office and quickly took in all of the accolades that filled his walls and shelves. It didn't matter if the award was from the Business Leaders of Antarctica, it was on display. His office was large, cornered, and filled with very expensive furniture that absolutely screamed, "I'm in charge here." I refrained from making any lasting judgments until we talked, but my curiosity was piqued. What unfolded next was somewhat surprising.

Chris slumped in his chair, which was strategically positioned ten feet away from his guest chairs on the other side of an imposing maple-wood desk, emphasizing the distance between us. With an exasperated sigh, he said, "I think it's me. I know you are here to assess the relationships of our teams and leadership, but I'm a problem." Chris continued to explain how he came to be CEO, how he was masking his insecurities with cockiness, and how the duality of his personalities was becoming debilitating.

Chris, one of the most intelligent people I've ever met, was insecure and anxious at his core. Chris had experimented at an early age to see what version of him people would react best to and found that pretending to be a jerk and braggart seemed to be an easier path to success than being an ambitious brainiac, even though the latter was more aligned with his soul. He remained surprisingly self-aware, and even if his vulnerability was tied to desperation, I appreciated it.

He was tired of pretending. He was tired of masking to appear confident and in charge. He wanted to *actually* be confident and in charge. He wanted to be a better leader. A better friend. A better partner. None of which was going to happen on a foundation built on fabrication. He knew his current approach to his business was going to tank the company and take him down with it.

NICK

Nick sent a message through my website after he saw my appearance on *Access Hollywood Live*. On the show, I gave advice to a couple trying to save their relationship, and the conversation hit a nerve. Nick had been with Hannah for a year and a half and wanted nothing more than to spend the rest of his life with her.

In the beginning, their relationship was easy and fun. They had late Saturday nights out and lazy Sunday mornings. They met each other's friends and families, and everyone got along. Hannah was everything Nick didn't know he was looking for, and everything he now knew he couldn't live without. The depth of his otherwise unnoticed emotions brought up insecurities he hadn't even known existed. Sure, his parents split up when he was ten, and his dad went on to start a new family 1,400 miles away, but he never thought about things like feelings.

Turns out our brains and hearts can conspire against us.

As Nick's love deepened, so did his fears of abandonment. His pain points were completely understandable, but those subconscious beliefs lead to very unattractive behaviors.

He started to smother Hannah, needing to spend every minute together, freaking out if she didn't reply to a call or text within moments, wanting to get married as soon as they finished school in spite of Hannah's preference for waiting until they were a bit more settled into their postgrad careers.

He was holding on ohhhhh soooo tight. And now she wanted nothing more than to break free.

His message to me was simple but heartbreaking: "I'm pretty sure I'm ruining my relationship. Please help before I've really fucked it all up."

Nick's abandonment by his father had left a confidence gap that had never been addressed or filled. His insecurities stemming from his father leaving were going to implode a relationship with lifetime potential.

KELLY

Kelly alternated between nervously sipping her wine and aggressively twisting the napkin in her lap. He was late. Maybe he wouldn't show? Could she be that lucky? Just as she fantasized about curling up on her couch in pajamas with a bowl of popcorn, her iPhone pinged with a message: "I'm so sorry. Traffic was insane. Parking now. Can't wait to finally meet you!"

Ugh. Why couldn't he have canceled and saved her the pain of another failed first date?

She had certainly had her fair share after her last relationship ended six months prior. Sure, her ex was unambitious, unfriendly, and unkind, but at least she didn't have to go on first dates during their year of domestic agony. It was what she deserved after all, wasn't it? It's not like she was that great a catch. Or so she believed.

To top off her rock-bottom self-esteem, Kelly had recently gained a few pounds from a hormonal imbalance. Fifteen pounds may be nothing on someone six foot five, but on her petite five-one frame, it felt like a hundred. While she would prefer to hide under a rock until her hormones decided to start cooperating again, at thirty-seven her biological clock created a deafening pounding between her ears. Hence, another date.

Mark entered the restaurant searching for a match to the photos on his app and landed on Kelly with an *almost* imperceptible furrow of his brow. He approached with a genuine smile. "Kelly?" Mark asked. She nodded and rose for an awkward hug. After an embrace akin to a thirteen-year-old boy forced to greet his great-grandmother, Kelly replied, "I know. I'm probably not what you expected," as she began nervously smoothing the parts of her dress that clung to her now larger hips and stomach.

Kelly spent the next ten minutes of the date berating herself and her appearance, explaining that while she's not normally super skinny, she's thinner than this, and she hadn't wanted to change her profile photos because she was afraid no one would want to meet her.

Mercifully, the waiter appeared to take their dinner order. "Have you decided?" Looking down uncomfortably, Mark replied, "I think we are going to stick with these drinks. Could you bring the check?" The sting of rejection reached Kelly's eyes, and they began to uncontrollably water. After the waiter retreated, Mark continued: "Listen, you seem really sweet, but I don't think this is going to work. I'm sorry."

"It's because of the way I look, isn't it?" Kelly replied.

"Actually, no. I get that you have gained a few pounds. It's honestly not that big of a deal. It's just that you seem really unhappy, and I'm not interested in dating someone committed to self-loathing."

Ouch.

Kelly knew there was no defense to Mark's statement. And she knew that it wasn't just her weight. Even if she lost the fifteen, she'd have found something else fundamentally wrong with herself that would prohibit a loving relationship. She was more committed to hating herself than her Netflix binges. This situation had played out before a dozen times, but no one had been willing to call her out on it until Mark.

Turns out that getting called out by a random internet date was just what Kelly needed to start making changes. After relaying the horror story to her best friend, who happened to follow me on Instagram, the Good Samaritan sent her my way. We had a bit of a road ahead of us, but as long as she was willing to do the work, I knew she could turn loathing into love.

HOW WE FEEL ABOUT OURSELVES IS HOW WE SHOW UP

From a bird's-eye view, these three stories are distinctly different. What could a CEO pretending to be a jerk, a boyfriend terrified of losing the love of his life, and a single woman sabotaging her dates possibly have in common?

Everything.

Chris, Nick, and Kelly all suffered from a confidence-shaped hole.

Many of us are dealing with these holes in our own lives. It consists of a hollowness created through circumstance, events, and/or environments—often unrecognized until its host becomes self-aware enough to recognize that their actions or reactions are being caused by a subconscious impulse. We pretend to be someone we aren't because we don't believe in our own (cap)abilities. We don't believe that someone will love us and stay with us because someone who loved us has left before. We don't feel worthy because we've been rejected in the past.

WHAT IS CONFIDENCE?

Psychological studies and philosophical discussions have swirled around the concept of confidence and self-esteem since the eighteenth century.[1] Confidence has been defined as an individual's belief that they are "capable, significant, successful, and worthy."[2] Oftentimes confidence is used interchangeably with self-esteem, which is identified as one's sense of worth and value.[3]

That's an important word, *worth*.

I am worthy. Just as I am. In spite of everything that I have gone through, everything I've experienced, and any lacking within my family of origin. In spite of every peculiarity I possess. In spite of any perceived flaw. I am worthy. That is true self-esteem. That is true confidence. However, in all of my years of working with humans, I've discovered that this is by far the most elusive feeling.

Chris, Nick, and Kelly all had experiences that resulted in a feeling of unworthiness. The results of an untreated confidence deficiency are understandable and common. I've been there myself and have traveled the journey from feeling unworthy to finally confident. It's impossible to go through life completely unscathed. A confidence deficiency will create barriers to happiness in every area of your life. The bright side is that building confidence is volitional and something you can work toward, regardless of the origin of the deficiency.

WHAT NOW?

You recognize that there is a confidence-shaped hole inside you. You may even know what caused it. You're committed to filling it. What do you do next? I'd like to introduce you to my confidence builder trifecta: the DFF. These are three techniques that when used in tandem can help to fill in that crater.

1. **Dig. Dig out the root.**
2. **Fake. Fake it till you make it.**
3. **Focus. Focus on your good.**

Let's unpack DFF.

STEP ONE: DIG OUT THE ROOT

You can't heal what you don't reveal.

–Jay-Z

Many authors choose to quote Descartes or Socrates. Me? I found Hova to be quite on point for this. If we don't dig out and learn to understand the root, we can never overcome the challenge. There will never be healing.

Imagine having a debilitating headache for sixty days straight. Not the headache you wake up with after one too many White Claws, or the one that arrives during allergy season that just wanted to hold hands with your runny nose and watery eyes. Instead, it's a merciless, pounding, all-consuming head-thumper.

The first week, you pop some Advil daily and assume it will pass. The next week, you switch it up to Tylenol because clearly the Advil wasn't doing it. The third week, you decide you really need to sleep more or cut back on caffeine. By week four, you'd better be making a doctor's appointment because there is clearly something below the surface that needs to be addressed. Something that needs to be dug up.

There are many techniques for building confidence that are like ibuprofen for a brain tumor. Maybe it'll take the edge off and help for an hour, but it isn't healing anything. We have to address the underlying source in order to develop real confidence.

Let's dig in. Here are some questions that can help with the excavation:

Think about your family of origin (your caretakers and siblings growing up). Was the environment supportive? Loving? Critical? Negative?

Was there a time in your life where you would have called yourself confident? When was that? When and why did it change?

What was your experience in school like? Did you have friends? Were you bullied? Accepted? Ignored?

Have you experienced trauma? Abuse can occur in many forms.

WARNING: It may be unwise to do this solo. This process can be messy, uncomfortable, and emotional. There are things you may dig up that need to be unpacked with the help of a mental health professional. Trust your gut. If you feel you could benefit from someone to work through this part of the process with, embrace that support.

Chris, our millionaire CEO, was quickly able to pinpoint where it all started. He was lucky to have supportive and loving parents, but his experiences in middle school left a deep gash in his self-esteem. His superior intelligence and natural ambition activated the often-overlooked inferiority complex of tweens. Chris wasn't naturally gregarious, funny, or charming, and so when he became a target, he withdrew instead of defending. He was ostracized for being who he was–smart and motivated–and consequently, his confidence took a hit. How could it not? Rejection of an immutable quality like appearance or intelligence can cut deep.

Nick's soil was similarly pliable. As a parent, I often joke that I haven't done my job right if my mothering doesn't land my kids in therapy. Just trying to support the industry. Dark humor aside, family of origin challenges are often the source of dysfunction in adults.[4,5] Nick was ten when his father left. Old enough to remember his mom crying in bed all day. Old enough to recall making his own "lunch" of stale pretzels and an orange with questionable fuzzy spots because grocery trips were far and few between. Old enough to remember that time he overflowed the washing machine because even he was repulsed by the smell of his clothes. Nick didn't know it then, but he was subconsciously associating a breakup with barely surviving. Who wouldn't be afraid to lose someone they loved, having had that experience?

Kelly's story started at home as well, though in my humble opinion her parents get a pass. It wasn't their fault they were physical specimens of perfection and she got the "I love cake" gene. I have that gene, too (and a penchant for pizza/beer/ice cream). Her parents loved and supported her regardless of her physical appearance, but with a mom who was an actual former runway model and a father who could stunt-double for Thor, it was nearly impossible to avoid the shame of comparisons. By puberty, Kelly realized that while she shared the same DNA, they did not share the same metabolism. She began to believe that she was simply less than comparatively.

Okay, I see it. Now what?

Maybe you identify with one of these sources of low self-esteem. Maybe you've uncovered your own. Now what do we do with it?

Acknowledge, accept, and affirm. *Acknowledge* that this happened and affected you.

"I experienced a trauma." *Accept* that you can't change the past.

"I accept that this happened and dwelling on the *what if* is not helpful." *Affirm* that you can change your present.

"Even though I experienced this, I can choose to react differently starting now."

As I mentioned above, some experiences may require the help of a mental health professional to unpack. I fully embrace and support therapeutic assistance in overcoming traumatic events of our pasts that impact our present and future.

In some cases, acknowledging, accepting, and affirming can be just the redirection one needs to dig it up and move forward.

STEP TWO: FAKE IT TILL YOU MAKE IT

"Fake it till you make it" is real. Of course it is—that's how Chris got in this predicament in the first place! He chose to emulate those he believed to be successful. Unfortunately, his sample pool was loaded with jerks. And

I can hear you now: *Wait, Rachel, didn't you just say earlier that we can't actually become better leaders/friends/partners on a "foundation of fabrication"?* That I did. As you may have gathered from what you have read thus far, I am a huge fan of authenticity and honesty. Chris was pretending to be someone he was *not* instead of owning who he is. In my practice, I encourage fake it till you make it to *own who you already are.* Worthy. And kinda badass.

Whether you deliberately strike a pose to invoke more authority,[6] choose power words in conversation,[7] or embody as a whole who you want to be and how you want to be perceived,[8] science backs you up. Act as if, and you can become.

Seeing as Chris had already proven this method, redirecting his course of pretense was a perfect prescription.

"Remember how you told me you purposely emulated those around you that seemed the most successful? Tell me how." Chris replied without a pause, "I studied them. I watched the way they interacted. I watched the way they walked. The way they spoke. I actually had a notebook where I would write down sayings they repeated often." He went on to explain that even though he knew they were jerks, he saw a clear benefit to their behavior—gaining success and respect. At least from a bird's-eye view.

"Perfect!" I squealed in a level of excitement that may have approached unprofessional. I calmed myself and continued, "Your ability to study and observe will serve you well."

I asked Chris to make a list of three people around him personally or professionally that he found genuinely confident and exuding high levels of self-worth. "Remember how you studied the other guys? Now you're going to study new subjects."

We recapped his findings two weeks later. Chris used adjectives like "calm, level, intelligent, humble, and objective" to describe his unknowing science experiment participants. "They don't take much personally. They know who they are and what they bring to the table." I asked Chris to create a crib sheet in his phone to remind him of the adjectives he would now embrace. Throughout the day he would reference his notes and remember that his only goal was to embody those traits.

It worked. Chris started to stand a little taller. He began to shift his interactions with his team from aggressive to engaging. He led with his intelligent opinions and created a space for dialogue. He texted me a month in, "This is easier than I thought it would be, but the biggest revelation is that it feels good. It feels like I'm just being me versus before when I was pretending to be someone else."

Fake it till you realize you *are* it.

You can utilize the approach that I employed with Chris to build your own confidence.

Who are those with unbreakable confidence around you that you can observe? What behaviors do you notice? How do they interact in conversations? How would you describe them? Use those observations to create your own crib sheet to remind you of your cues throughout the day. How can you show up in your life by acting more _____, _____, and _____?

The more you step into your worth and act as if you are confident, the more the world around you will reinforce those feelings within.

BE THE BALL

The fake it till you make it approach can also be supported with thoughts and visualizations. I'm a huge proponent of meditation, but I'm not a sit on a mat and clear my head kind of meditator. Clear my head? I wake up with questions. I go to sleep with plans. Clearing my mind always felt like an unattainable goal, which is why I embraced hypnosis with a giant bear hug.

Hypnosis is meditation with a goal attached. You enter that blissful meditative state where your arms and legs feel like lead, but you are focused on visualization and reprogramming your subconscious versus clearing your mind. There are many techniques for hypnosis, some led by a hypnotherapist like me, and some you can employ solo with minimal experience.

In the case of Nick, I taught him a quick trick to calm himself any time he felt anxious about his relationship. I asked, "What is your favorite memory of you and Hannah?" He replied, "When we went on our cross-country road trip. We took two weeks off and had no plan other than to end up in California." He was practically gushing about how adventurous and exciting it was to choose their next destination each night and have karaoke contests during the drive. They had never felt more connected. "How did you feel when you were on that trip?" I asked. "Happy, content. I felt like we could handle anything, and I knew there was nowhere else she wanted to be." I told him how absolutely perfect that memory was, and that we needed to re-create those feelings. Nick was under the impression I was asking him to take another road trip.

"Uh, Rachel, I don't have another two-week vacation right now." "You don't need it," I replied. "You can go there in your mind. And other places, too." He stared at me like most people do when my more "woo" side comes out.

"Here's what I want you to do, each morning before you get out of bed: Take a few moments with your eyes closed to just breathe. Take ten full breaths, all the way down into your belly, and hold each for a count of five, and then release all the air in your lungs.

"After those ten breaths, I want you to imagine yourself back in that car. See your hands on the steering wheel. Feel the air blowing your hair around. Feel the smile on your face. Bring yourself back to that trip with every imagined sense. Look over at Hannah and see her smile back at you. Take a few minutes to feel good in that moment.

"Then imagine yourself later today doing something mundane. Eating dinner. Walking the dog. Cleaning up the kitchen. Something you do together, but now, attach that emotion from your trip. Those same great feelings. That same level of connectedness you felt. Spend five to ten minutes on this exercise every morning and then go about your day."

"That's it?"

Admittedly, Nick was skeptical. I wasn't asking him to really *do* anything differently. Thankfully, he was willing to try anything, at least once. Three weeks later my phone pinged:

"I can't believe I'm typing this, but that shit works."

He had done the exercise most mornings and had only spent on average seven minutes doing so. Even halfheartedly, his visualizations had improved his confidence in his relationship tenfold.

"It made me feel so much more peaceful. Just remembering how happy and connected we were made me realize how happy and connected we can still be if I just relax."

So try it out. You can visualize anything. Start with a great memory from your past when you felt amazing, and then transfer those emotions to something you will do in your present or future. Imagining yourself more confident in scenarios can translate into actual confidence when you live out that event in real life.

It may have been a while since someone handed you a paintbrush and a blank canvas for your life, so asking yourself, "What would my life look like if I was truly confident?" can help to get the creative juices flowing. Run through those scenarios in your head. Feel the feelings attached. See how people react to you being so confident. Take a minute each morning to simply imagine those scenarios, and I promise it will not only feel amazing in the moment, but start to play out in real life. I've included a self-hypnosis track on my website to guide you through this process.* It'll start by helping you get into a meditative state (even if you've never meditated before) and then walk you through the process of bringing to mind a great memory and transferring those positive emotions to a situation in the present or future. You can use it as often as you'd like depending on how quickly you see results. I try to encourage using it daily for at least a week. I mean, it's only ten minutes and you get my "hypno-voice"! Totally worth the investment of time.

STEP THREE: FOCUS ON YOUR GOOD

In my first meeting with Kelly, she had no problem telling me about everything she did wrong and everything she hated about herself. "My body hates me. I'm stuck in a job I hate. I'm terrible at relationships." *Welp.* That's one internal dialogue that can't be hidden with great foundation and a sweep of blush.

I then asked her to tell me something she loved about herself and something she did well. Her face slacked and her shoulders slumped as the silence blared.

"Nothing."

"Nothing? No way. There is *something* that you like about yourself. Everyone has something. What about your sense of humor? Your fashion sense? You are incredibly kind and caring. I would shave your amazing hair and wear it like a wig." The last item was unnecessary.

She laughed. "I guess you're right. I'm not all bad."

You may be surprised, but this exchange is pretty typical. We humans are extremely adept at recognizing our flaws. Ask anyone, even those with healthy self-esteem, what they would change about themselves and you'll get a list longer than a woman looking for her unicorn soul mate. I would

---

*   https://www.racheldealto.com/self-hypnosis

like to think that I now have a healthy level of self-confidence, and I could still name ten things in an instant that I would change about myself physically, emotionally, or intellectually. In contrast, it is often very difficult for people to identify and embrace their strengths.

What is confidence but owning your strengths? We aren't likely amazing at everything, but we are amazing at *something*. In order to build confidence, you need to create your highlight reel and play it often.

"I want you to sign up for a class in stand-up comedy and find somewhere you can do volunteer work that aligns with your passions. I know you don't have limitless free time, but if you can allot one night a week to cover both activities, I'll be happy." And obviously my happiness is paramount here.

Kelly fought me unsuccessfully. She eventually acquiesced and found a beginner's class for stand-up and a local Dress for Success organization to offer her services. She texted on a break from her first class: "I may resent you forever for this one."

Ah, the message you have always wanted to receive from your client.

The next day, Kelly updated me: "Okay, so the first hour *was* painful. I wanted to crawl under the dilapidated theater seats and die. But then we played an improv game and I was GOOD. I was laughing so hard after that my eyes wouldn't stop tearing. Everyone kept high-fiving me. Ugh. I hate to admit it, but I actually loved it by the end of the night."

Kelly went on to take the two next levels of stand-up classes. While she still has no desire to actually become a professional comedian, she found herself addicted to the high of doing something *well*, and she had FUN!

What do you do well? What is an asset you can focus on and enhance? Try this simple technique to boost your own confidence.

Create a list of three things you do well:

_____

_____

_____

What can you do to enhance each attribute?

_____

_____

_____

THE LAST WORD . . .

We could spend the rest of our lives focused on what we could do better, or we could give ourselves permission to celebrate and enhance what we do well. Everyone has something. I watch a lot of fashion makeover shows, and unlike the HGTV shows I am obsessed with, you can't just tear down parts of a person and rebuild. You need to accentuate the positive—a proportionate figure, great hair, big eyes, etc. Think of this aspect of the DFF as a makeover show where you find a great part of you to coat with mascara.

LET'S DO THIS!

ACTION:

How would you describe yourself? How would your loved ones describe you?

_____

_____

_____

What do you believe is standing in between you and your most confident self?

_____

_____

_____

How can you show up differently using the FF of DFF? How can you embody your most confident self and focus on your best attributes?

_____

_____

_____

MINDSET: I am enough.

Chapter Five

CONNECT—POWER OF POSITIVITY

MICHELLE

Michelle arrived home from work with the intensity level of a Category 5 hurricane. Her partner Tom had hoped it would have been downgraded to a tropical storm in the hours since he had to make that dreaded call but no luck. Michelle remained quite the force.

"What do you mean we didn't get the dog? You *know* how much that puppy meant to me!"

"Uh, babe, you didn't even know the dog, how could it have meant so much? We'll find another."

You didn't have to know Michelle well to recognize that that was entirely the wrong response.

"ARE YOU KIDDING ME?! Did you see his eyes?! He was perfect. And now everything is ruined and we'll never find our dog. I should have expected this. Things never work out for me."

Michelle started slamming cabinets in preparation of her nightly cocktail, leaving Tom to stare at his hands awkwardly and wait out the anger. He was unwilling to share any voice of reason or note that there are almost 90 million dogs in the United States and that the odds were in their favor for finding a pet.

Tom was going to sleep on the couch for this one, and he knew it. At least in Michelle's eyes, it was obviously his fault that another applicant was chosen over them. Tom knew Michelle wasn't going to get over this for some time. All over a puppy she never met and a process they had no control over. Tom found himself reminiscing back to when he had found their home. It boasted an open layout, beautiful woodwork, and lush landscaping. It was everything they had always wanted but never had in their

New York City pad. Tom was so excited for Michelle to see the place that he was barely able to contain himself until they could walk through it with their Realtor. He knew it was perfect. "Wait until you see the kitchen; it has everything on your list!"

Even with a Viking stove and enormous island, a scowl reached her face the moment they pulled into the perfectly paved driveway, and it never abated. Michelle picked apart everything she could in every room, crushing Tom's enthusiasm with each criticism. In the end, she remarked, "It's awful, but it's better than the others we've seen. I guess we can make an offer. I'm still disappointed you couldn't find what I wanted." She gave him the cold shoulder for three weeks after they closed. At least he had amazing crown molding to keep him company.

Anyone observing this situation would wonder why in the world Tom was with such a melodramatic brat. He was such a good guy, levelheaded, kind, and with a huge heart. Tom was the guy that helped a friend move on his birthday and called his mom at least twice a week to make sure she felt loved. Michelle, though, found a problem with everything, with lost puppies and imperfect houses only a sliver of what set her off.

The thing was, Michelle hadn't always been this way.

Tom and Michelle had initially met in college. Tom was an undergrad who enjoyed the parties but still managed to get his classwork done, while Michelle was a highly ambitious pre-law student, and a member of a sorority known for being low-key and fun. They didn't actually "date" in college—uh, does anyone?—but spent a lot of time "hanging out" together. After graduation, they ended up living in the same New York neighborhood. Tom began his entry-level job in finance, and Michelle started law school. They became inseparable and far more serious about their relationship, moving in together after six months, and getting engaged a year after that.

It wasn't one particularly traumatic event that changed Michelle, but a series of smaller happenings that resulted in her evolution into pessimism. To begin with, she had a harder time in law school than she anticipated. Michelle was always able to remain at the top of the curve as an undergrad without much effort, but in law school, *all* of her classmates were top-of-the-curve students, making her, well, average. Michelle had never been average. Her ego sustained a significant hit and her stress levels soared. As a law school graduate myself, I've always remembered the saying, "What do they call the person at the bottom of their law school graduating class? An attorney." Michelle didn't share my pragmatism.

Michelle spent two years post-law school grinding out eighty-hour workweeks for a boss she resented. How often could one take a three-hour lunch and dump responsibility on their associate? Turns out, often. She practiced in an area of law she didn't enjoy, lived in a city she had no time to explore, and had a new husband she never saw. On top of it, her sister, to whom her mom had compared her for all her life, led a seemingly idyllic existence with her perfect house, ideal job, amazing husband, and beautiful new baby.

Stress and FOMO accumulated until Michelle could only see how terrible her life was. Nothing made her happy. Alleged problems were everywhere. Out of an innate survival instinct, Tom began to master the art of walking on eggshells.

The move to the suburbs was essentially an unlabeled intervention. Tom, becoming more and more stressed by his wife's constant negativity, thought that if he found their ideal house and she changed jobs, he would get the "old Michelle" back.

"All she needs is a breather. More free time, and more space," he explained to his friends after a night filled with friction. Michelle, not a fan of the restaurant he picked for dinner, decided to storm off before dessert. "I don't know, Tom, maybe *you* need space more than she does." Maybe his friends were right.

Tom reached out to me in a Hail Mary attempt to save his marriage. They now had a great house and Michelle had a new job with better work-life balance, but misery persisted. It was as if she *preferred* kvetching. Her marriage suffered, her friends had all but disappeared, and she remained trapped in a tornado of negativity. The spiral was killing their relationship, and without an intervention, it seemed doomed.

Can you imagine Tom meeting Michelle *after* she went to the dark side? There would be no Tom and Michelle, or Michelle and any other person who valued their happiness, for that matter. Her friends had all but abandoned her, unwilling to expose themselves to the soul-crushing irradiation of her gloomy life outlook. Her job was safe at least, because . . . lawyers.

I have never encountered someone who was drawn to a negative person. Negativity is the antithesis of being relat*able*. A negative mindset can contaminate every interaction, connection, and relationship. Take a moment to think of someone you have recently engaged with who seemed negative. They may have complained often and for no reason, the scowl on their face perceptible and permanent. I bet it took less than sixty seconds to recall how quickly you wanted to exit the conversation.

Now think of a time you were connecting with someone who was a positive-minded person. Positivity is when you can look at yourself, your life, and your future with a positive outlook.[1] Those conversations may have been filled with a combination of hope, encouragement, and optimism. Interacting with a positive person can feel like sunshine on your face with an appropriate SPF. You want to be around them, because instead of feeling depleted, you feel fulfilled. We are drawn to positive people, and as a positive person we can draw others in and become more relatable. Being positive is not only beneficial for your relationship building, it's beneficial for *you*. Positivity can help you live longer,[2] prevent heart attacks,[3] have a more successful career,[4] and boost immunity.[5] Not a bad ROI for looking on the bright side.

NEGATIVE CAN BECOME NORMAL

If positivity is so awesome, why isn't everyone spewing rainbows? Likely if one was given a choice, they would choose to be positive, but often people end up in a position similar to Michelle's. Exposed to a series of events and environments, they become increasingly negative. The more negative one becomes, the more difficult it is to lift yourself out, just like quicksand. (PS, I was today years old when I learned you can't really die in quicksand.[6] Mind blown.) Regardless of fatality risk, negativity growth is exponential and dangerous in many other ways.

Michelle is an excellent example of what I find to be a fascinating function of our brains, neuroplasticity. *Neuro-what?* Good news! Your brain is like Play-Doh. Bad news, it probably doesn't smell as good. Man, I loved that stuff as a kid.

"Neuroplasticity can be defined as the natural tendency of the brain architecture to shift in negative or positive directions in response to intrinsic and extrinsic influences."[7] In other words, our reactions to our environments shape our brains and determine how positively or negatively we feel. Your brain is malleable, in either direction. Research has shown that what we repeatedly focus on creates stronger neural connections, and then those connections make us think those thoughts even more.[8] It can be a vicious cycle when those thoughts are negative.

I find the easiest way to explain this concept is by imagining your brain and its thought patterns as a series of highways. Some roads are well paved, and others consist of dirt and gravel. In a generally positive person, their paved roads represent their positive thoughts. As most of their thoughts and beliefs are positive, those roads are driven on way more, and with each pass those roads get smoother and smoother. However, in Michelle's brain, and the brain of any more negatively minded person, the most traveled and smoothest roads represent her negative assumptions and beliefs. As your brain will always prefer to drive on the smoother, well-paved road, the more positive you are, the easier it is to stay positive, while unfortunately, the same holds true for the negative.

Are we forever resigned to a life of negativity if our neural pathways are a smooth blacktop? No. Let's get back to those dirt roads, the ones that represent positive thoughts in a presently negative mind. Can our brains ever explore them? They sure can, but you have to turn the wheel.

Remember how Michelle wasn't always negative? She was a far more positive person but had turned that wheel over and over again, choosing to focus on the negative until her more positive pathways became dilapidated and rocky like a neglected New Jersey highway, while her negative pathways became smooth like butter. Michelle is proof that our Play-Doh brains can change, though not always for the good.

In order to rewire her brain in the right direction, Michelle, and anyone else negatively minded, needs to get her hands back on the wheel and get off her destructive autopilot settings. More good news? There are proven therapeutic methods that can help you change those thoughts and take control of paving those roads.[9] If you believe in your ability to control your thoughts/emotions and create a supportive environment for positivity to thrive, you can step out of that negativity tornado.[10,11]

Here is my three-step process for becoming *positively* rela*table*:

- **Step One. Set your positivity baseline.**
- **Step Two. Assess your environment.**
- **Step Three. Create awareness and spin.**

STEP ONE. SET YOUR POSITIVITY BASELINE

Everyone loves a good before and after! This isn't exactly a *Biggest Loser* weigh-in, but if you don't know where you start, how will you know how far you've come? Many of us are unaware of how positively or negatively we naturally think. Minus a significant level of self-awareness and a psych degree, we assume that however our brain works is the "normal" way.

Enter the Positivity Scale, an assessment created by scholars that can help to quickly check out where there is room for growth.[12] Take a look at these questions, and jot down your answers, which can range from 1 (strongly disagree) to 5 (strongly agree).

- I have great faith in the future _____.
- I am satisfied with my life _____.
- Others are generally here for me when I need them _____.
- I look forward to the future with hope and enthusiasm _____.
- On the whole, I am satisfied with myself _____.
- I feel I have many things to be proud of _____.
- I generally feel confident in myself _____.

For each response, the closer you are to a 5, the more positive you are in that area. Fives across the board? You can pretty much skip steps 2 and 3. You are rainbows and unicorns personified. Go throw your glitter on people! However, if you are like the rest of us mere mortals with areas of improvement, you can utilize your scores to see where to focus your efforts. We're going to get into the "how" of that in Step Three. After six weeks of implementing the next two steps, I'd love for you to revisit this scale and re-rate yourself to see areas of improvement.

STEP TWO. ASSESS YOUR ENVIRONMENT

It's a heck of a lot easier to become more positive when your environment supports good feelings! In my first meetings with Michelle and Tom, we discussed their history and the series of events and circumstances that led them to their present situation. "Michelle, it sounds like you were generally happy until you started getting hit with stress meteors. That job alone sounded like hell. It's understandable you were affected." I was purposely validating her so that we could try to skip the defensive stage, but it was also accurate: Michelle's environment played a huge role in her current negative state. "I guess it's true," she replied, "everything was easy until I graduated college. After that, it's all been downhill."

"What would you have done differently?" I asked. She answered that law school was a nonnegotiable as becoming a lawyer was her dream since she was little, but she'd have chosen a different job. Michelle knew the moment she stepped into the interview that her boss would be a nightmare to work for. Her (unfounded) feelings of lawyerly inadequacy that developed in law school resulted in her accepting the first job she was offered. Remember that person you dated for a bit even though you knew you should have run from the start? That guy with all the red flags you ignored? Yep, it was exactly like that.

"Okay, so your job was a huge part of what made you miserable, but what about your feelings about your sister? Or how stressed you were about not having time with Tom? Or just time?" I asked. Michelle looked frustrated. "I don't know, I don't see how I could have changed any of that." While some of Michelle's challenges involved undeniably negative influences, others were created by her perceptions of the situation. It was time to take a look at and categorize what was affecting her.

We have two piles that we can toss our environments into:

- **Gotta go**
- **Gotta change**

Gotta go. In some cases, we can change our environment because we have a choice, meaning that we can choose who we spend time with, where to work, and where to spend our time. Michelle's job and boss had an enormous negative impact on her. Spending eighty hours a week being taken advantage of while working in a small windowless office with an undersized desk surrounded by stacks of files marked "URGENT" could lead to a breakdown in anyone. Michelle was lucky and in a different position than many. Her husband's job could have supported them both temporarily until she found a new gig. It wasn't necessary to stay in that awful environment.

Michelle had a double whammy: The job was terrible on its own, but her boss was equally awful. Sometimes it's solely the person. You may have had an experience where the job was great, but the management left much to be desired. Or the manager was fine, but your colleagues were horrible. The people you spend time with (willingly or not) have an enormous impact on your positivity. If you're trying to adjust a negative mindset, it may be necessary to look at your colleagues, friends, and family from a lens of "is your effect on me positive or negative?"

You may have heard the saying, "You are the average of the five people you spend the most time with." Originally coined by a motivational speaker, this was also supported by a neuroscientist who found that two people spending time together ended up having almost identical brain waves.[13] Those Play-Doh brains are at it again! Seriously, though, how many people around you would you really want to match waves with?

Are there people in your sphere of influence who are negatively impacting you? Take a look at your roster and see where you may need to re-evaluate your starting lineup. Sometimes you can avoid them. I have people in my life that I avoid. Not necessarily because they are bad per se, but because I can feel the depletion of my happiness level when we spend time together. When talking with them, I'm exhausted after a phone conversation. A coffee results in forty-five minutes of life sucking. God forbid we grab dinner, because I'd be ready for bed at 8 p.m. Wait, that's every night. I digress . . . There are simply people who don't deserve your orbit, and in fact are damaging the way you show up in the world. Whether it's the job you should leave, the person you need to avoid like Covid, or a physical environment you need to change up, it's *gotta go.*

If you can let it go.

But Rachel, I can't quit my job/avoid my mom/break my lease?

Yep, sometimes reality gets in the way of my *gotta go* pile, too, which is why we also have . . . *gotta change.*

Gotta change. What happens when it's gotta go but you can't actually get rid of it? Or maybe you don't want to get rid of it? If we can't eliminate what's affecting us, we need to change the situation *or* how we react to it.

Michelle knew law school was nonnegotiable. Even though her alleged mediocrity stressed her out, she would never have dropped out, and I would never have recommended that she do so. She was in it for the long haul, and while she couldn't change the fact that she was surrounded by students smarter than her, she could change her perspective of the situation. Michelle had the opportunity to appreciate the opportunity to learn from being around extremely bright people. Instead of comparing and feeling inferior, she could have connected and found some great study partners. Or she could have viewed being among intellectual superiors as an honor. It would have required a coming-to-terms talk with her ego but there is an opportunity in humility. Perception is everything.

"Tell me about your mom," I prompted. "What about her?" she replied quizzically. "In our talks, it sounds like your problem isn't with your sister herself, but the comparison your mom has always made between the two of you." A floodgate of memories opened, with many supporting the notion that her mother had unfairly pitted the two sisters against each other in every arena, including academia, popularity, and success. "But she's my mom." Many of us, like Michelle, have had to come to terms with the re- alization that sometimes we have to look at our closest relationships with more realism than roses.

People we love can have a negative impact on us.

People who love us can be a negative influence.

Depending on the situation, difficult decisions may need to be made. I've worked with people for over a decade, and I've heard so many stories that I now tend to think of (and write about) with caveats. There are times when your loved ones are toxic, and the only way to eliminate their ef- fect on you is by eliminating them from your life. Only you can assess how harmful the relationship is, and as always, utilizing the help of a mental health professional in these situations can be extremely beneficial. We will discuss this area further in Chapter Eleven: "It's Not You, It's Them."

There are other situations, though, that we *can* change. In many cases, like Michelle's, we can address the negativity and work to find a way that our loved ones remain a part of our lives, but without the nega- tive impact. In order for Michelle to let go of the negativity of her mom's criticisms, I encouraged her to start by expressing herself and setting boundaries with her mother. "Let her know how the comparisons have affected you and what they have done to your relationship with your sis- ter. Help her understand that if she continues to put you down and com- pare the two of you, that the conversation will be over." Michelle wasn't looking forward to standing up to her mom, but she did so soon after and was shocked at her mom's reply.

"She started crying. She had no idea that she was being so critical and didn't realize it bothered me. Apparently, her mom did the same thing to her, always pitting her against her brother." Was her mom perfect thereafter moving forward? No, but Michelle was able to call her out lovingly when she slipped back into old behaviors. Understanding the origin of her mom's actions also helped to temper Michelle's emotional response, as she now knew her mom didn't *intend* to hurt her; she was simply stuck in a cycle.

Not every situation is as easily remedied as Michelle's relationship with her mom. In some cases, the conversations may be difficult or entirely unproductive. You may need to limit the time you spend with certain people or set strong boundaries. Every relationship is different but know that every negatively impacting relationship does have a huge effect on your positivity, and your happiness is worth the attempt to change.

In addition to facing challenging relationships, we can also be stuck in a physical place. Like that time I was trapped in an apartment from hell. I was a young mom of a three-month-old baby, living below two sumo wrestlers with a penchant for practicing their skills at 3 a.m. Or at least it felt that way. As someone who values sleep over pretty much everything, I was miserable. My neighbors were unempathetic and my landlord unwilling to let me move early. I was convinced the stress would break me. I found myself snapping at loved ones, having less patience with my son, and failing to be productive. It was 100 percent a negative impact on my positivity.

I had two options. One, I could focus on how awful the situation was and cry into my pillow at night, or two, I could find a way to survive those remaining four months with minimal pillow wailings. Instead of searching for voodoo dolls in the shape of my tormentors, I reminded myself that my neighbors had as much a right to be awake at 3 a.m. as I had a right to be sleeping. I napped more. I bought earplugs and played white noise. I visited my parents' home often. I changed as much as I could to lessen the impact. It wasn't perfect, but it was a choice, and I survived.

The **gotta change** pile requires acknowledging what we can control, what we can't, and taking all possible actions to change the impact of that negative circumstance.

Where is your environment affecting you?

What piles have you made?

How can you actively quash negative influences in your world?

STEP THREE. CREATE AWARENESS AND SPIN

We have a *lot* of thoughts. In the time between my writing of this book and your reading of it, another conflicting study will likely have been published. Even if we assume the more moderate estimates, we have about 6,000 thoughts a day.[14] That's a lot of thinking! No wonder I'm exhausted all the time. Our (6,000) thoughts have an enormous impact on our psyche, especially as those thoughts are highly repetitive (remember, paved roads). Positive self-talk can be uplifting and confidence boosting, while negative self-talk can create a gloomy cycle that becomes difficult to break. Embracing our ability to take control of our thoughts and feelings, we can begin to shift that negativity. How do we take control of those negative thoughts? We need to create awareness and spin.

First, we need to become aware of our negative thought patterns. Have you ever bought a car and then everywhere you look, all you see is your model and color car? No, there wasn't suddenly a run on gray Toyota Priuses (unless you live in Southern California). You are now more *aware* of that particular car because of your purchase. The same number of that particular car was in circulation yesterday, but you weren't paying as close attention. We find what we look for and awareness begets awareness. So, what if we started to look for our own negative thoughts?

I had Michelle start a negativity journal, one of my favorite methods to employ when helping clients become more aware of their negative thinking. It's a version of a technique that has been utilized for decades and has even been prescribed as a performance enhancer for athletes.[15] She loved it from the start. Okay, not so much.

"This is dumb. I haven't used a diary since I was ten," Michelle complained.

"Amazing! Write that down!" I replied, undeterred.

Michelle's complaint, accompanied by an impressive eye roll, was her first entry: *This is dumb and it won't work.*

"Now what?" she asked. "What is the opposite positive thought of 'This is dumb and it won't work'?"

Journaling my negative thoughts will be helpful.

"Perfect! Now do that for every negative thought that pops in your head." Michelle groaned. I gave her a pass on that one.

Over the next two weeks, Michelle filled ten pages of her diary, er, journal. It shocked her how many times she thought negatively–about herself, her life, her work, her marriage.

I look like crap.

I never have enough time.

Everything is hard for me.

I will never really be successful.

Tom doesn't care about me anymore.

Michelle realized that many of her negative thoughts were repetitive day to day. Her roads were like freshly pressed asphalt that a kid would love to bike on. "It's almost embarrassing seeing this on paper" she admitted. "How do you feel, though?" I asked. "Honestly, it's made me realize how shitty I've been to be around. I wouldn't want to hang out with me, either. I want to change." We then went over the ways in which we would work to spin those thoughts:

"I look like crap today" became *"My hair looks great today."* Note: This worked because it gave her something positive to focus on even if she couldn't get to "I look great!"

"I never have enough time" became *"I am in control of my time and can fit in what I prioritize."*

"Everything is hard for me" became *"I am capable."* Note: One could change this to *"Everything is easy for me,"* but my goal is always to find a phrase that you can truly get behind and believe; Michelle wasn't there yet.

"I will never really be successful" became *"I am already successful. I am thankful for everything I have."* Note: Gratitude is *such* an important element of positivity. Anytime you can include a statement of gratitude to counter a negative thought, you are winning.

"Tom doesn't care about me anymore" became *"Tom loves me enough to work through this bump."*

It really started to shift for Michelle after four weeks of journaling and spinning. Her entries decreased, and her overall demeanor shifted. "I didn't believe that this would work, and I one hundred percent never thought I'd start to believe the new thoughts." I told her to go write that down. She laughed. I wasn't kidding.

The negativity journal has been one of my most successful techniques for helping clients recognize and shift their thoughts. It's simple but effective, as it's based on everything we know about the brain. I promise you will love it. Eventually.

Let's get you set up to start your own negativity journal.

1. **FIND A JOURNAL:** Yes, an actual physical journal. I know it's easier to use your phone, but studies show you are far more connected to your writing when it is by hand.[16]
2. **START TRACKING:** Write down your negative thoughts as they occur.
3. **SPIN 'EM:** Every thought has a potential counter thought. Choose a counter thought that you can get behind. Bonus points for gratitude.
4. **STAY CONSISTENT:** Ideally you will use your journal until your positive thoughts outweigh your negative ones. We can't get our ideal body after one workout, and we won't shift our negative thinking without consistent effort.
5. **TRACK YOUR PROGRESS:** Oh boy! Another before and after. I told you I loved them. Take a look at your week-to-week decline in negative thoughts. Observe what areas are improving.

Even the most resistant find themselves evolving with the negativity journal. It's a practice that you can come back to at any point where you feel like your negative thinking is beginning to outweigh the positive. Isn't it incredible to recognize how powerful you are?

THE LAST WORD . . .

Positivity is not only a key element to achieving relatability; it makes it so. much. easier. Michelle was able to save her marriage by shifting toward a more positive way of thinking, but maybe your situation isn't so dire. Maybe you want to be able to deal with a tough situation or difficult person.

Maybe you want to be happier. Maybe you want to make connections more easily. Creating a baseline with the Positivity Scale, changing what you can within your environment, and taking control over your thoughts will have you becoming positively gleeful.

LET'S DO THIS!

ACTION:

Where do you have the most room for improvement on the Positivity Scale?

_____

_____

_____

What areas of your environment can you change to support your positivity?

_____

_____

_____

Get journaling!

_____

_____

_____

MINDSET: I see the good in everything.

Chapter Six

COMMUNICATE— PRESENCE OVER PRESENTS

The second element necessary for becoming more relat*able* is communication. It's impossible to write a book on relationship building without including communication skills as a major component, and there are quite literally thousands of books and articles written by other experts that give great tips and strategies to make you a better communicator. In all those thousands upon thousands of words, I often find something missing, though. Communicating to *truly* relate to other people is an energetic act. It's alive.

We spend so much time focusing on the how-to-talk that we forget how to just *be*. There are only two things you need to remember to be a great, relat*able* communicator. You need to be present and you need to be adaptable. Our presence tells someone that we are all in. We are committing all of our attention and energy to making sure that the person we are communicating with feels our focus. Our adaptability allows us to adjust our communication to meet our audience (whether one person or one hundred) where they are.

With that, let's dive into **presence**.

"The deepest urge in human nature is the desire to be important."
–John Dewey

Have you ever struck up a conversation with someone at an event and immediately *knew* they were somewhere else entirely? Their eyes drift away, you're constantly asked to repeat yourself because they aren't listening, and they check their phone often and conspicuously. Oh, technology, how I love thee, but it's amazing that something designed to keep us connected keeps us so apart.

I will be the first to admit that I am addicted to my phone. I often feel unfairly judged by Apple's Screen Time feature but seeing the hours I spend each day on my phone does nothing to change my habits. The moment my eyes open in the morning, I sleepily reach to the left and feel around until I find my beloved six ounces of metal. I then spend at least twenty minutes checking notifications and scrolling Instagram with one eye open before finally getting up to indulge my other addiction, caffeine.

One night I was watching a movie with my daughter during a school break. In my preemptive defense, we had spent the past week together, 24/7; we did things, went places, and hosted her friends for playdates. I mommed hard. Now it's twenty minutes into *The Incredibles 2* (for the tenth time, mind you), and we each have a hand in the over-buttered (is there such a thing, though?) popcorn. In spite of practically knowing the script verbatim at this point, my daughter is fully engaged and laughing. Me? My lone unbuttered hand is simultaneously shopping on Amazon. I'm buying things I don't really need and definitely don't need in two days.

She turned to me with her beautiful giant brown eyes and said, "Mom, can you put down the phone and watch this movie with me?" Ugh. The holy guilt/shame shower. My kid called me out on something *I teach to other people*. I was making her feel ignored for what? A sale on vitamins that I'll never take? To quote the invitation I received for a friend's birthday party, "Your presence is my present." While we all know she's lying and actually wants gifts, the premise is accurate.

In all relationships, be they budding or fully formed, our presence is the greatest gift we can give. My daughter is stuck with me. I will have a second and third (and thousandth) chance to get it right with her. We don't always have that much room for error.

You have one shot in an interview.

You have one shot on a first date.

You have one shot meeting a potential client.

You have one shot at a first impression.

Initial connections with anyone require your A-game. And if you want to continue to build that relationship? You have to continue to bring it.

What if we practiced presence and "being here now" in our daily interactions?

We've all been there. We can all recall that time we were with someone that we wanted to grow a relationship with, professionally or personally, but we weren't quite present. You were thinking of something else or perhaps someone else. You simply weren't there. There are a million excuses as to why. I know you had a lot on your plate! It was a stressful day, you got that distracting email, there was so much to do when you got home, your mom won't stop calling–I get it. For a moment though, imagine going back and making different choices. Imagine being fully present. What would you have done differently?

BE LIKE FRED

I'm going to date myself here, but I grew up with the most amazing man. No, not my dad, though he was amazing to grow up with, too. I'm talking about Mr. Fred Rogers. His PBS children's show *Mister Rogers' Neighborhood* was a staple in my house. He had soft-spoken confidence and exuded kindness and compassion. He was the ultimate example of what it means to be a good human.

When I read Maxwell King's *The Good Neighbor: The Life and Work of Fred Rogers*, I found myself intrigued and even more appreciative of the man behind the show. I've seen how those in show business aren't always consistent on-screen and off-screen, and it was comforting to learn that Fred Rogers remained the same man when the cameras stopped rolling. King included a story in the prologue that perfectly demonstrates how to be really truly present, and it has stuck with me since first reading it.

In 1985, at the height of his show's success, Fred Rogers was invited to appear on *The Oprah Winfrey Show* (also an iconic staple of my youth). The entirety of *Mister Rogers' Neighborhood* was dedicated to helping children feel and understand love, kindness, compassion, and acceptance. Which is why it was odd that Rogers insisted that there were absolutely no children in the audience at Oprah. No kids allowed when his entire at-home audience was children? Odd. Or self-aware. Fred Rogers knew that if there were kids present, he would be more focused on them than on Oprah.

TV doing what TV does, the Oprah producers ignored his request. It makes sense from a producing angle: if you book a famous children's television personality, kids in the audience are a natural part of the segment. They didn't quite understand what they were getting into, though, further evidenced by their decision to allow the kids themselves to ask questions.

"As soon as the children started to ask him questions directly, he seemed to get lost in their world, slowing his responses to their pace, and even hunching in his chair as if to insinuate himself down to their level."[1] A little girl ran up onstage for a hug, which he happily provided. A boy concerned about the setup of the miniature trolley onstage had Rogers's undivided attention. In an instant, Fred Rogers became far more concerned with making sure every child felt heard and seen. Creating good TV for Oprah was an afterthought. The segment was derailed by an innate proclivity toward being present to who mattered most.

The moral of that story? If Fred Rogers can ignore Oprah and be present with a little girl who wanted a hug, I can ignore the ding letting me know my vitamins are on the way.

Unfortunately, we don't all look good in a red cardigan sweater, so let's dive into how we can all be a bit more like Fred Rogers in our connections. Presence can be accomplished by focusing on these three elements:

- Eye contact
- Eliminating unnecessary distractions
- Curious listening

EYE CONTACT

Mark was a coaching client of mine for two months before we met in person. Based in Texas, he had been referred by a mutual acquaintance to help with his sales skills. He worked remotely for a software company and felt that his growth had stagnated. I'm not an ABC (always be closing) sales trainer, but I have worked with many organizations to help their teams create better relationships in order to sell more. It's all . . . related (pun fully intended). In two months together, we had made some progress, but he hadn't achieved the kind of breakthroughs I had hoped for. "My email interactions with clients are great now, and I find myself far more confident and connected on phone calls. Something happens in person though, and I don't know what it is, but things seem to go off the rails every time," he relayed.

At this point, I was curious as to what could be so different in person when he was having success via email and the phone. Bad breath? Disheveled appearance? Second nose? I'd seen pictures and we had FaceTimed, so I was pretty sure he presented as "normal." "Aren't you in NYC for a conference next week? Let's have our session in person and do a mock client interaction," I offered. He agreed.

Mark walked into the coffee shop with a crisp suit, combed hair, no detectable odor, and a single nose. So far, so good. He sat down in front of me after we greeted each other and began to look at the menu. And then he looked at the menu some more. And then his eyes proceeded to dart from mine to something clearly more interesting behind me, then the floor, the ceiling, and his coffee.

"Uh, Mark? Got somewhere else to be?"

"No, why?"

"Your eyes are all over the place. We're having a conversation here and it feels like you'd rather be anywhere else."

There it was. Something so simple. Mark excelled behind a screen or a phone, but once he was in person, he was completely disconnected. "It just feels so awkward. I guess I never realized how much I avoided it," Mark surmised.

Eye contact is absolutely vital in any social interaction. A direct gaze builds connection and communicates that you're present.[2] We all have had a conversation with a Mark and know how it feels when someone won't meet your eyes. You inherently feel less connected. You question their character. You wonder why you're wasting your time on a conversation they aren't interested in.

The desire for eye contact is innate and biological. Studies have shown that even days-old newborns prefer faces that make direct eye contact.[3] In four-month-old healthy babies, their brains show "enhanced neural processing" with a direct gaze, which means that eye contact gets the motor of their brain spinning.[4] Like babies, eye contact is fundamental to get our processes up to speed.

But I don't wanna.

I agree with Mark, eye contact can be awkward! At dinner the other night I was intensely stared down by a toddler. She was cute and all, but I'm pretty sure she was judging me for failing to return that library book in the sixth grade. It was really intense. Making and maintaining eye contact can feel uncomfortable and vulnerable for anyone. It's intimate and can make you feel a little too . . . *seen.* I will not often disregard your feelings, but when it comes to eye contact? We've got to get through this hurdle. It's that important. In order for someone to feel your presence, you must begin to practice good eye contact. We need to look one another in the eyes when having a conversation in order to build that connection.

To be clear, this doesn't equate to a creepy stare-down without a break in connection. Research has shown that overly intense eye contact can feel uncomfortable and overload the brain.[5] Most people are uncomfortable after nine seconds of sustained eye contact, so it's important to find a balance between "I am paying attention" and "I am stealing your soul."[6]

Here are some dos for maintaining eye contact in conversation:

- **Do** hold eye contact the majority of the time while talking.
- **Do** take breaks after five to six seconds of mutual gazing.
- **Do** practice a visual "wander" when you break eye contact versus focusing on something else in the environment (that is, don't break eye contact to actively watch TV or stare at someone else; let them float unfocused).
- **Do** maintain even more eye contact while listening versus speaking.

As with everything else we have been discussing, shifting our habits is a process and patience is necessary. It took Mark about a month of interactions before he began to feel more comfortable naturally making eye contact in conversation, and as expected, his in-person sales improved. You can do this.

ELIMINATING UNNECESSARY DISTRACTIONS

So many distractions, so little time. We can't be present if we are paying attention to something else other than the other half of our conversation. When's the last time you phubbed someone? Or have been phubbed? I admitted to phubbing during my movie night with my daughter and it was not okay.[7] Phubbing (phone snubbing) occurs when we snub those whom we are talking with to look at our cell phone instead, a growing phenomenon in a world where we are all attached to our devices.

Not surprisingly, phubbing has been shown to negatively impact relationships and communication.[8] If I'm in a conversation with someone and they keep looking at their phone, I'm going to think they aren't invested in this conversation, and therefore I shouldn't be, either. Being snubbed for a phone can make you feel excluded and rejected.

Admittedly, it's not always Steve Jobs's fault we ignore one another while communicating. We can also become distracted by our environments or other elements in our periphery. Anytime you pay more attention to what's around you versus what's in front of you, you are damaging your relationship's potential. I once went on a date with a former pro baseball player. To a sports bar. During baseball season. As we walked into the bar, I could sense that he was really excited—for the three games playing in high definition. That night I learned more about Linda the bartender's life than my date's. We never went on a second.

There will always be an opportunity to become distracted during conversation, but there is no easy fix. You have to make a choice: them or that?

Do you choose to focus on the person you're talking to or your phone?

Do you choose to focus on your date or the TV?

Do you choose to focus on the person you're chatting with or are you keeping an eye on the bigger fish you want to network with at the event?

The goal in being present is to be there in that conversation both physically and energetically. Eliminating unnecessary distractions means that we develop tunnel vision for the person we are engaging with. Whether it's a phone, television, or other people, we need to be strong enough to resist the urge to multitask. When in doubt, ask yourself, "How would I feel if the roles were reversed?" and then think of my daughter's shame-inducing eyes. Focus.

CURIOUS LISTENING

I unabashedly started eavesdropping on the pair seated three seats down. I was engaged in one of my favorite activities while traveling solo for work, people watching at the hotel bar. It's not snooping, it's research. My bar tab is a write-off.

The raven-haired beauty was enamored with her date, and likely herself as well. She was smiling and making eye contact but spending an equal amount of time checking out her hair and makeup in the mirror behind the liquor shelf. It was great lighting, she looked gorgeous, and it all made me giggle in my malbec. We humans are so entertaining.

I overheard her date say, "I had a chance to go to Italy this past year, it was amazing," a perfect opening to ask questions about his trip, but she replied with a five-minute monologue of all her amazing travels through Europe. He asked appropriate follow-ups, and once they exhausted her passport stamps, they moved on to work. "So, what do you do?" she inquired. I'd have preferred a little more finesse with the question, but at least she asked one! He began to tell her about his work as an analyst and she nodded with a forced smile. "That's great," she replied unenthusiastically. No further questions. No interest. No energy. This uninspired banter (though could you really call it that?) continued for another twenty minutes, and as they ordered another drink, it took everything I had to not scream "Run, dude! She's a dud."

Honestly, it was zapping my energy just watching these two. That's not what conversation should *feel* like. Sure, she was making eye contact and her phone was away, but she wasn't invested at all. A little curious listening could go a long way.

Uh, Rachel? I think you mean "active" listening.

Yep. I know. Active listening is the gold standard in communication. Active listening involves paying complete attention, showing interest in what the speaker has to say, and engaging verbally and nonverbally in a way that demonstrates you've been paying attention.[9] It involves incorporating both of our previous steps, eye contact and eliminating distractions, but also involves focusing attention on your responses.

I want you to do *all* of that, but I want more. I'm pretty demanding. You should know that by now. In addition to paying attention and showing interest, I want you to get curious. Imagine the difference in conversation between the couple at the bar if she practiced curious listening?

He says: "I had a chance to go to Italy this past year, it was amazing."

She says: "Wow! I haven't been to Italy, but spent a ton of time traveling Europe. Where did you stay? Was the food as amazing as they say it is? Tell me everything!"

Or when it comes to the job talk:

She says: "So what do you do?"

He says: "I'm a financial analyst."

She says: "Ah, I have to admit I have no clue what that involves! What does your day-to-day look like?"

He says: "It's a lot of researching and making recommendations on stocks. I work for a financial firm, and while it's a lot of number crunching and reading, I love it."

She says: "It's great that you love what you do. How long have you been in the business?"

Can you feel the difference in the conversation? The actual convo was flat and dull and the only thing keeping their connection alive was a physical attraction. The ideal conversation creates a potential for something more. That is a relationship-starting conversation.

It works in every interaction, not only on a first date. Anytime that you connect with someone, whether it be the first or fiftieth time, you can be a *curious* listener.

Here are three steps to becoming more curious in conversation:

1. **LISTEN FOR TOPICS THAT INTEREST YOU:** You may not be curious about everything they say, but if you are paying attention, you will be interested about something. Find a topic that you can relate to and that you would like to learn more about.

2. **ASK OPEN-ENDED QUESTIONS TO INSPIRE STORIES:** The hardest part will be refraining from sharing your story on the topic versus inspiring them to share their own. We often relate by talking about our own experiences, that is, "I broke my arm a few months ago and it's crazy how long it takes to truly heal" is often met with, "OMG I broke my arm in the fourth grade. It was awful. I couldn't swim all summer." That's not a conversation strengthener, that's self-interested. Focus on "how, what, why," like:

   • How did that happen?
   • What led to that decision?
   • Why did you choose that direction?

3. **IMAGINE YOU'RE RESEARCHING A STORY:** If you're a good reporter, you don't stop after the first response. Ask follow-

up questions that genuinely interest you. Let one story weave into the next.

"I broke my arm a few months ago and it's crazy how long it takes to truly heal."

"Wow, how did you do that?"

"I was mountain biking and hit a rock. I flew over the handlebars and my radius broke my fall."

"Ouch! I broke my arm once, too; it was awful. How long have you been mountain biking for?"

"Since I was twelve. My dad used to take me. He passed away last year, and now I ride for him. I'll be back on my bike next week."

That's a curious conversation. It didn't take much to get to a deep story that can help build a real connection.

Still not convinced? Take a genius's word for it: "I have no special talents. I am only passionately curious." Einstein. Curious listening ftw.

THE LAST WORD . . .

I still want presents for every holiday, but presence really is a gift. The more that we can focus on maintaining eye contact, eliminating unnecessary distractions, and engaging in conversations with curious listening, the better connections we will build. You have the ability to be present in every interaction, and your presence will make you undeniably relatable.

LET'S DO THIS!

ACTION:

Where can I create device-free zones in my life?

_____

_____

_____

How can I become more curious in my conversations?

_____

_____

_____

MINDSET: I will be present in every interaction.

Chapter Seven

COMMUNICATE—
FLEX YOUR
ADAPTABILITY

"It is not the strongest of the species that survives, nor the most intelligent. It is the one that is most adaptable to change."
–Charles Darwin

Have you ever walked into a group of people intending to say one thing, but you quickly realized whatever you had prepared was going to go over like a lead balloon? Maybe you've been in a conversation and things weren't jiving because you felt like you were on different pages. Or perhaps there was a time where your timing was frankly terrible. In Chapter Six, we discussed the first half of rela*table* communication–presence–but now it's time to dive into the second and equally important component, our adaptability.

The most interesting aspect of human relationships is also the most frustrating, which is how incredibly different we all are. I used to say we are as unique as snowflakes but given how that term has taken on a political connotation, let's go with humans are unique as . . . fingerprints. We are composed of so many different facets of personality, experience, environment, and mood. No two people are alike, as all of these elements shape every interaction.

Due to these differences, there is no one size fits all for relationship building, and never let anyone tell you differently. It elicits a face palm when I see books/articles/media trying to script conversations, that is, "Say this to make them buy from/hire/date/love you." As if there were a formula that transcends all of our uniqueness?! I wish there was. I'd be out of a job, but it would save so many from those awkward, uncomfortable, and frustrating moments. While those resources could be great jumping-off points for some, they should never be considered gospel and copy/pasted into your life and communications.

There is no one line. There is no one approach. There is only your adaptability.

You may be asking, "Why do I have to adapt? Why don't they adapt to me?" Here's where I give you some tough love. If you want something, you do the work. If you're the more emotionally intelligent person in the situation, you do the work. If you want to be a better communicator, you do the work. Adaptability can help you connect, build, and support relationships and help you get what you want, whether that's a connection, a sale, a promotion, or anything else that requires interacting with another human. So like, a lot.

Our adaptability in communication is our ability to change based on **environment**, **temperament**, and **timing**.

SAVE THE ENVIRONMENT

Mike walked into his first company meeting at his new job with a yet unearned bravado. He slumped lazily in a chair toward the back of the fluorescently lit conference room and rolled his eyes as his team leader began to describe recent research on a medication his new employer manufactured. "Can we get on with this so I can go make some money?" he said under his breath. Unfortunately, Mike's inside voice had failed him yet again, and his new colleagues cast disapproving sideways glances. They were invested. They lived, ate, and breathed this company and his pomposity wasn't making him any friends.

Mike was in theory a perfect specimen for a pharmaceutical sales representative. He was confident enough to walk into a doctor's office without an iota of nervous energy and had a gift for being able to have a conversation with anyone about anything. He was a hit with his offices and had a roster of receptionists that would roll out the red carpet for him at a moment's notice. He left his previous company when he was recruited with the promise of more money and better benefits.

In Mike's previous job, the sales team consisted of reps with equal levels of narcissism. Those meetings were more akin to a locker room before a football game, and motivation was valued over education. He was under the impression that this company culture would be similar and believed sliding into an apathetic role would connect him with his colleagues.

Perhaps it was the 7:30 a.m. start time of the meeting and the lack of coffee coursing through his veins, but Mike had failed to recognize the difference between the atmospheres. He didn't notice his coworkers sitting upright and focused on the presentation. He ignored the way two associates eagerly asked follow-up questions and how the rest of the room actually cared about the answer. He ignored every cue and showed up the way *he* wanted to show up. To his great disadvantage.

You have one chance to make a first impression, and while you can certainly work your way back from a bad impression, it's a heck of a lot easier to put the effort into the initial interaction. Mike was surprisingly humbled pretty quickly. After the meeting, the manager who had hired him pulled him aside to say, "Hey listen, Mike, I think you have a lot to bring to the team, but we are collaborators here. Not agitators. I'm not sure what the climate was like at your last job, but it's not going to fly here. Your numbers won't save a bad attitude."

It had been some time since Mike had been anywhere near reprimanded by a supervisor. He knew at that juncture he could choose his ego or his success. Thankfully, Mike valued this opportunity more than saving face. He promised to change his behavior and apologize to the presenting partner. He learned a somewhat embarrassing lesson in pliancy that day.

You've likely heard the expression "read the room." However, the ability to read the room isn't always easy. The ability to perceive emotions is an art form, but one that is an indispensable component of communication. In order to be more relatable to his new colleagues and bosses, it was vital that Mike learned to acclimate to his new environment. That doesn't necessarily mean he had to become someone he wasn't. I would never expect Mike to return to the next meeting with enthusiasm to learn, but it's important that he at least shows up neutral. Recognizing that we aren't in sync with our environment is half the battle; the other half is determining how we can show up and still feel authentic, which sometimes involves more observation than interaction.

What about when we already have a relationship with the person? What happens when we steamroll our way through those interactions without regard to the environment? There are times when the actual content of our conversations needs to pivot as well.

Take Bridgette. She had recently had the most magical adventure in Peru. She climbed Machu Picchu, did yoga with adorable baby goats, and felt completely transformed after two weeks away from her stress-filled job. Bridgette and her good friend Allie had made plans to meet for lunch before her trip, and Bridgette couldn't wait to fill Allie in on all of her experiences.

As Bridgette arrived at the restaurant, she was bursting with anticipation and sat down at the table with the excitement of a five-year-old on Christmas morning. Before her friend had even looked up from her menu, Bridgette started rambling, "Omg, you *have* to go to Peru. I feel like I am still flying from how amazing it was. The people. The food. The hikes. It was *magical*. I don't even understand how people could live their whole life and never go. That is tragic. I think I'll even go back. Maybe more than once! Want to come next time? You would love it! You could even bring Jack."

Bridgette must have prattled on for five minutes straight before she even really *saw* her friend sitting across the table; until that moment Allie was simply a body she could gush to. Finally, Bridgette took note of her muted friend. Allie was on the verge of tears, and with one "Wait, what's wrong?" from Bridgette, the floodgates opened. While Bridgette was having a magical goat-filled adventure, Allie's boyfriend had broken up with her, and she had been completely blindsided. Bridgette felt awful for her happiness bombing. Allie felt awful that Bridgette didn't recognize her melancholic state. It made for an awkward rest of the lunch.

Bridgette recalled this scenario to me in a session. I asked her why she wanted to talk about it, and she said, "I felt really bad, but I didn't know how to save the conversation. She's still upset with me." To which I replied, "Do you care about Allie as a friend and her feelings?" "I do. She's a good person and a great friend." I told Bridgette what I would tell anyone in that situation: if a friend (or frankly anyone) is upset, the entire conversation has to be refocused on support of that person. Regardless of the relationship, what you are trying to say while someone is upset will never land. It's an environment you may encounter in your personal, professional, and romantic relationships. People get upset. Sometimes at you. Sometimes about something completely unrelated to you. The response is the same. There may have been something else on your agenda to talk about, but in that moment, it's far more important for the sake of that relationship that you focus on them. There will be another opportunity to make your point, ask your question, or tell your story.

There are limitless situations where we will need to adapt to an environment by learning to read the cues of others. Every interaction can benefit from giving yourself the flexibility to adapt to possible connection killers like mismatched cultures and emotions, as was in the case of Mike and Bridgette.

TAKE A TEMPERAMENT CHECK

I don't know about you, but I've never had my forehead shot as many times as I did in 2020. While temperature checking is a helpful assessment of health, temperament checking is a way more helpful way to assess our approach in communication.

We all know the golden rule, right? "Treat people the way you want to be treated." On the surface it seems legit. If I want to be treated with respect, I should treat others with respect. If I want someone to be kind to me, I should be kind to others. Makes sense.

Adaptability takes the golden rule to the next level. We have to treat others the way they *need* to be treated. It's treating someone with empathy and understanding, which goes a long way in relat*able* communication. What is empathy anyway? It's important to define here, as it often gets confused with sympathy. Sympathy is "I feel bad for you," while empathy is "I feel you." It's when you understand what someone is going through and imagine what it feels like to be them.

Think about the very widely discussed personality trait of extroversion. Extroverts love a good party, they get fired up being around people, and have a minimal need for alone time. On the flip side are our introverted friends. They require quiet time to regroup after spending the day in groups. They may skip the after-party. Some could be labeled as "shy" or "reserved."

What happens when an extrovert approaches an introvert with no regard for their feelings or need to ease into a conversation? A complete and utter disconnect occurs. Their feelings of discomfort are often visible and palpable. They stop smiling. They create physical distance. They eliminate eye contact to try to reduce the intensity. They create as much of a divide as possible.

I have a very extroverted friend, Natalia, whom I adore. She is always the life of the party and handles the spotlight like no one else. Natalia's a "Johnny One Note," though. She is always "on" and barrels through conversations. As an extrovert, I can handle Natalia. However, I have seen many a potential connection be put off by her personality. She only embraces one way of being, and in spite of the ability we all have to adapt, she chooses not to. I've even had gentle conversations with her after witnessing a particularly awkward encounter. Natalia replied with a shrug, "Love me or leave me." It's entirely her choice, but it's likely that her success will be stilted by her inflexibility.

Gauging the temperament of the person allows us to get a feel for who someone is before we steamroll a conversation. It can avoid a gaffe that may get in the way of building a relationship. When in doubt, listen more and talk less until you know how to meet them where they are.

SET YOUR TIMER

Your adaptability to the emotions and personalities of others will take you far, but what happens when it's simply a matter of timing? Like with Bridgette's lunch disaster, her friend wouldn't be distraught forever. Allie was having a moment in time, and in order for Bridgette to connect with her friend, she needed to change her approach to the conversation. Sometimes, the conversation shouldn't happen until the timing is right. It reminds me of a time I had a big ask, and it could have gone either way.

The fact is, I won the parent lottery. I grew up in a home where my parents loved and respected each other. They have been together since the first day of freshman orientation in college and still clearly love each other half a century later. It's also always been evident that they loved me. They are my biggest fans, and I'm not only telling you this because they will read this book. In all honesty, if I end up in therapy, it won't be because of my relationship with my parents.

I was an awkward and dramatic thirteen-year-old in a house of sports fanatics. Quite literally, everyone in my family excelled in sports, except for me. There was my dad, a basketball coach and former ball player himself, my mom, a track star, and my brother with his killer three-point shot. Me? In middle school I'd remain on one end of the soccer field with the argument, "They're going to come back. Why would I run down to the other side?" I tried every sport at my parents' behest and repeatedly proved my inadequacies and disinterest regarding anything to do with rubber balls.

I did love something, though. Performance. There was nothing more I wanted as a teen than to quit the pretense that I had any athletic ability and audition for a play at a local community theater. The show was *Alice in Wonderland* and it was being produced at a tiny dark hole-in-the-wall space pretending to be a theater in a town twenty minutes away. It could have been a front for a child kidnapping ring, but I didn't care–the prospect of being a part of the show was everything to me.

There was a problem, though. I was thirteen and unable to get there on my own. The show and its rehearsals were during tax season and my dad is a CPA, which meant he was out of the house twelve-plus hours a day due to an inflexible government deadline. The daily drive to and from the theater would fall entirely on my mom, who also worked full-time *and* did everything around the house. Bless my undomesticated dad, from whom I've inherited much. My mom, though? She's basically Donna Reed with an apron and a lawn mower and a career. It was a big ask and I was terrified of being shut down.

The first night I went to bring it up, I walked into the kitchen to the sounds of slamming pots and heavy sighs. Mom was exhausted. She had likely chopped down a tree and rescued an orphaned puppy earlier that day, and now making dinner was the last thing she wanted to do. Well, no, the last thing she'd want to do is agree to take on a two-month daily commitment of driving me back and forth to do this play. I backed away slowly, retreating to my room until dinner. You may be wondering why I didn't offer to help her with dinner, but really, I wanted us all to live. No one needs me in the kitchen.

The next day, I woke up to sunshine, chirping birds, and a mom who was ecstatic because it was Saturday, with no office to go to and a day full of weeding the yard ahead. (Don't ask, it's her happy place.) I plopped down at the breakfast nook table, and as she sipped her coffee, I led with "Hey, Mom? There's something I'd really love to do. Something that I would rather do than anything else."

Her positive response was likely because she wasn't fully caffeinated yet, but she did in fact say yes. While neither of us really knew how intense theater would turn out to be, in that moment, she was excited for me. For the next four years she took me to auditions, rehearsals, and performances without many breaks between shows. While she did so willingly, I can tell you that woman was not upset when I got my license and could start driving myself.

Often, the difference between a yes and a no is timing. And far more often than that, the stakes are higher than a teenage girl wanting to join the theater. How many times do we force the timing of conversations because we want the discussion to happen immediately versus waiting for a more appropriate moment?

My mom would have said no if I had asked on the first night. Granted, I may have been able to persuade her when she was in a better mood, but why get off on the wrong foot if I can be patient? Forcing the issue would have stressed us both out.

Think of all of the situations in which this could apply:

- **You go to close a deal and the client is irritable and frustrated over a staff issue.**
- **You need to talk to an employee about constantly coming in late, but they're focusing on an important project.**
- **You want to ask for a raise or promotion and your boss is more stressed than usual.**
- **You want to have a "talk" with your partner, but they're on deadline for a project.**
- **You want to ask someone out, but they seem uncharacteristically distracted and aloof.**

There are times you may feel like if you don't have that conversation as soon as possible, you could burst. It's not always easy to muster up the patience and wait until the right moment, but if you can, it can have an enormous effect on the outcome.

THE LAST WORD . . .

Communication is both nuanced and simple. In every situation, the most important consideration is to stay tuned in. We often listen in preparation of replying, but if we listen with the intent of adapting, our entire demeanor changes, and we create far more possibilities to form relationships. Many times, the difference between a yes and a no is timing. The difference between a positive conversation and a negative encounter is being able to read your audience. The difference between making a good impression on someone and sending them running is being able to meet them where they are.

LET'S DO THIS!

ACTION:

Describe a time when you missed the cues in a conversation.

_____

_____

_____

What could you have done differently?

_____

_____

_____

How can you be more adaptable moving forward?

_____

_____

_____

MINDSET: I am aware of social cues.

Chapter Eight

COMMUNICATE— WORDS MATTER

"We need to talk."

Vanessa's heart dropped into her stomach as she read her boss's text. She needed this job. She was good at this job. She knew the numbers were down in her area, but she had a plan to raise revenue and rebuild her team. Didn't her boss see how hard she was working? She dialed Jason's number with a trembling thumb, saying a silent prayer that her voice wouldn't convey how scared she was to have this conversation.

"Vanessa! How are you today?" Jason bellowed. Vanessa, convinced he was trying to make her feel comfortable before letting her go, swallowed nervously, took a deep breath, and replied, "I'm good. You wanted to talk?"

"Yes. It turns out Marie in the southern district is pregnant. She's planning on taking an indefinite leave. She gave her notice today," Jason explained.

Vanessa, confused, replied, "Oh wow, that's a huge territory. I'm surprised she would give that up."

"Well, she is, and I want you to take it over. I'd like you to keep your territory if you think you can manage both. You're going to need to hire more staff," Jason explained.

Uh. What?! Vanessa was trying to process the emotional swing from being convinced her boss was firing her to . . . receiving a promotion? "Yes. Yes. Absolutely. Thank you!" she stammered. Vanessa was surprised she could even speak given how fast her heart was racing. Her hands were still shaking as she put down the phone. She stared out the window in disbelief. It took another hour before she was able to find a regular cadence to her breath. What a roller coaster!

We've spent a considerable amount of time talking about the energetic component of communication. The presence that is required to ensure that someone knows you are there and eager to connect. The adaptability that is necessary to create the best outcome in any conversation. We now have to think about the actual words we say.

Word choice matters.

Have you ever had a positive reaction to the phrase "we need to talk"? I know I haven't! The expression typically connotates something bad–breakups, firing, disappointment, anger. Those four words lead to nothing but stress in any relationship–personal or professional. They should be removed from our vocabulary.

What could Vanessa's boss have texted that would have limited her anxiety spike? While he could have called from the outset so Vanessa could gauge his tone, he also could have written:

"Hey! May have a great opportunity for you–let's talk."

"Around later? I have a possibility to run by you."

"Need to fill you in on some internal changes. Could be good for you."

Any of these three would have let her know that the conversation was likely to be positive. Vanessa's future cardiologist would be immeasurably thankful for an alternate selection.

In every conversation, whether via text or in person, we have an opportunity to choose words that connect. Our goal as part of the conversation should be to allow the other person involved to remain open and engaged. Vanessa showed up to that phone call stressed! Her heart was beating so loudly that her brain was barely functioning. She was in fight-or-flight mode, and she was flighting. In those instances where our stress levels rise unnecessarily, we are far less able to engage in meaningful conversation.

How we engage is directly relational to how others are able to engage with us. The words we choose can alter any conversation. Our goal, when aiming to be relat*able*, should be to put the other party at ease. Our word choices matter whether we already have a connection to someone, as Vanessa had a professional relationship with her boss, or are meeting someone for the first time. Even with small talk, it's imperative that we choose words that connect rather than terrify.

I had the pleasure of keynoting at a marketing conference in person right before Covid-19 struck. Much of the audience consisted of executives in a variety of industries looking to grow their businesses and further develop their in-house marketing departments. I've spoken at events like this before and always enjoyed connecting with the audience after my talks, as they are typically attended by smart and creative people. This event was no exception. The coffee break after my speech was filled with a terribly burnt medium roast but also interesting conversations with attendees from all over the country. A woman approached me as another conversation naturally came to an end. "That was a great speech," she said. "I normally hate the keynote speaker, but you were actually decent." Um, thanks? I recognize that she was attempting to compliment me, but it didn't actually feel . . . good.

"Thank you. What brings you to this conference?" I asked, brushing off the odd statement.

"My boss sends me every year. I only go to the sessions because he makes me report back on what I've 'learned,' which is nothing. But I like the free trip."

All righty then. I had a feeling based on her initial comment that she and I wouldn't be clicking, but like I said, there are always such interesting people at this conference! I really wanted to give her a chance to redeem herself and see if she had anything else to share other than complaints.

"Gotcha. Well, I better head out, I have a flight at two p.m."

"Ugh you're so lucky. I wish I was leaving."

I ran from that conversation. The natural happy high I always feel coming off the stage was dwindling fast in her presence. Granted, her energy was extremely important, and she needs to read my chapter on positivity, but everything she said could have been tweaked to avoid an adverse reaction.

Let's go through how that could have played out differently. We'll call her "Woman" because I fled that convo so fast, I didn't even catch her name:

Woman: "That was a great speech. I really enjoyed it, and I've seen a lot over the years!"

Me: "Thank you! What brings you to this conference?"

Woman: "My boss sends me every year. I'm an account executive at a small advertising agency in Oregon, and he likes to keep up on marketing trends. I have to say I love the trip; Chicago is a great city."

As you can see, I didn't change much, but it changed everything. All of a sudden this is a person you want to keep talking to! I have so many questions for this new version of "Woman," like, what does your agency focus on? What do you love most about Chicago? What session are you most looking forward to? The gist of her comments to me didn't change and she's not faking excitement to be there, but her replies don't send me running, either.

Our goal, especially with initial conversations, is to make the other person *want* to keep talking to us. Small changes in word choice can make an enormous impact on how welcome they feel in the conversation.

So how do we choose words that promote connection? We get some ESP!

Really, Rachel? You expect me to be psychic to communicate better? While some otherworldly skills could help us out in this area, I don't expect you to be able to read minds. What I do expect is that you can become **empathetic**, **straightforward**, and **positive** in your word choices.

EMPATHETIC

As we have learned, empathy is an enormous part of any successful communication. In the last chapter, we discussed empathy in relation to treating people the way they need to be treated and how we can show up energetically to match the state of the person we are connecting with. In this section, our focus is on how we can ensure that our word choices land in a way that best serves the relationship. As before, the more that we place ourselves in the shoes of the recipient the more we can connect.

Imagine if Jason had thought about how Vanessa would perceive his "we need to talk" text. His is especially egregious because it's pretty universal that "we need to talk" = bad. Or at least it should be. If he had thought about Vanessa's reaction, he would have recognized that the recipient of a text like that might become anxious or concerned. Unless he was into psychological warfare, two seconds of thought added to his communication could have saved Vanessa a boatload of stress.

You may be thinking, *What's the big deal? It all turned out okay.* You're right, the end result was Vanessa got a promotion. However, the PTSD of that text remained. For months following that day, every time she saw her boss's name pop up on her screen, she flinched. Why risk altering the strength of a relationship when two seconds can prevent the damage? Our goal in all relationships is to build them up.

In order to be an empathetic communicator, we need to take a breath and think before speaking or texting. When sending text messages and emails, we have the time to assess our language and to confirm that they support our intent. In face-to-face communication, it becomes a bit trickier. If you spend two minutes thinking through each reply, your partner in conversation may become confused or tap out entirely. We can become an empathetic communicator on the fly, but it will take practice. Before asking a question or replying, try taking a beat, think of how your words will land, and then say them. The more often you practice taking a second before opening your mouth, the more it will become second nature.

I had a client who never thought before he spoke. Dan was always "super busy" and barked at his staff as opposed to talking with them. He truly felt that he didn't have time to slow down and think before he opened his mouth. Have you ever met someone who just vibrates with that kinetic energy who perpetually looks like he just took eight shots of espresso? How the heck do you get someone like that to slow down? With Dan, it took looking at his dismal employee retention rate. He was losing money through employee turnover, and he started to question if he was the reason.

"What is your goal here?" I asked, over a strong latte that wouldn't make me a tenth of how wired this guy was. "To increase our profit and improve efficiency. These projects are taking too long," he replied. The challenge was that his business was creative. His team was far more artistically inclined than numbers savvy. He had been yelling at them to rush a process that they deemed sacred.

So I asked, "You were a designer once. How would you feel if you were yelled at to rush the process?"

His response? "I'd be pissed."

I explained that he could ask for the same thing, but he had to do it differently. He needed to think of how his words would land before he spoke and choose words that encouraged his team and respected their art but also allow them to recognize the balance that needed to be achieved between art and business. It took practice, but even taking a breath before losing his temper made a huge impact on his word choice. He began to use phrases like, "I understand what you are aiming for here. It's awesome. We need to figure out how to deliver the drawings on time. How can we do that?" A question instead of a bark allowed Dan's team to buy in to the solution. He still shakes with caffeinated energy, but he breathes a lot more.

Always think before speaking/typing/writing.

Ask yourself: "What words can I choose that will convey my message in a way that's best for this relationship?" Practice makes almost perfect (because perfect doesn't exist).

STRAIGHTFORWARD

Our word choices should almost always be straightforward. Sure, there are times when you can be coy or use innuendo, but we can save those for after-dark flirtations. Our goal when deciding what to say should be to relay it in a way that the message is clear.

You are likely familiar with the four basic styles of communication: passive, aggressive, passive-aggressive, and assertive. In order to communicate in a straightforward manner, our goal would be to be assertive as often as possible. Let's observe the difference in word choices between the four styles with the example of this sentence: I want my roommate to bring home a pizza.

A passive communicator focuses on the needs of others at the expense of themselves, they don't stand up for themselves, and they often get walked over. A passive choice of words to get that pizza home would include something like:

> **"If it's okay, it would be great if you could bring home a pizza. If you can't, though, I can do it. You know what? I'll do it. I've got it."**

Cringe-worthy. I don't know about you, but it made me feel uncomfortable simply reading it. That person may not have much respect for themselves, and they're creating a relationship where they are not valued.

An aggressive communicator is the opposite of passive. Their needs matter above all. They are disrespectful, forceful, and a bit of a bully. If one were going to ask for that pizza in an aggressive way, they would say:

> **"I don't care what you have going on, you better pick up a pizza on the way home. I'm already hungry. You better not be late with it. And it better be hot still."**

Equally cringe-worthy! The recipient of aggressive word choices is immediately put on the defensive. These are not relationship-building words.

Passive-aggressive communicators are unique animals. They seem passive on the surface, but they use word jabs to express the frustration they feel they cannot directly express. Here's how they would ask for that pizza:

> **"It would be great if you could bring home a pizza for once. You probably won't, but it would be nice if I wasn't always paying for your food."**

Jab, Jab. Hook. They clearly have something to say and a grievance to air, but they'd rather go for the guilt.

Finally, we get to assertive. Our gold standard. An assertive communicator stands up for their own needs but also recognizes the needs of others. They ask for what they want and express their opinions in a way that is respectful and confident. Here's how they would ask for that pizza:

> **"Hey! Can you grab a pizza on the way home? I have cash here for my half. Thank you!"**

Clear and concise. Not demanding. Respectful. Straightforward.

All of our conversations can benefit from straightforward dialogue. Clear communication allows the receiver to remain open to conversation. As you can see from the above pizza examples, the other styles can result in the recipient developing negative feelings about the conversation and person. A simple change in word choice can invoke feelings of defensiveness, lack of respect, anger, and frustration. None of them lead to relatability.

Take a moment to reflect on your most common style of speaking or writing. You can even scroll through your text messages and emails. Does your style change based on the relationship? Perhaps with a boss, you are more passive. Maybe you have a toxic ex with whom you are aggressive. There could be moments that you respond to your mother's passive-aggressive tendencies with your own jabs. We're all human, after all. How can you work toward being more assertive and straightforward in all communications?

POSITIVE

Didn't you write a whole chapter on positivity? Do I really need more?! Ya sure do!

We can often say essentially the same things with a more positive choice of words, which makes a world of difference. Negative word choices are another way we shut the door on connection, while when we choose positive words, it allows the conversation (and relationship) to continue. Using positive words in conversation makes us more relat-*able*.

In every conversation, there is an opportunity to create a more positively worded experience. See the chart below of some common phrases in conversations, both at work and socially. First, read down the list of all the negative phrases. I don't know about you, but none of these scream to me, "You are totally someone I want to talk to more!" Now read the positive spin on those sentences. You can say the same thing without a negative emotional impact.

NEGATIVE	POSITIVE
When are you getting here?	Looking forward to seeing you, what's your ETA?
I can't.	I wish I could.
What is wrong with you?	Are you okay?
Are you done with that yet?	When will that be done?
Don't do it like that.	Let's try it like this.
My boss is such an ass.	My boss is a bit of a challenge.
I am so stressed out.	I have a lot going on, but I can handle it.
Don't you understand this?	Let me know if it makes sense.
I guess I can go.	I'd love to come.

Remember the negativity journal you started in Chapter Five? You began tracking your negative thoughts and spinning them into affirmative statements. You're likely already seeing a decrease in your negative thought patterns by becoming aware of those thoughts and spinning them. Think of this section as introducing a live-action version of that journal.

Instead of the thoughts that circulate in our head, we're recognizing the words that come out of our mouth.

- **Step 1:** Become aware of the words you say
- **Step 2:** Identify when you say unnecessarily negative words
- **Step 3:** Choose positive replacements

Similar to the journal practice, this can take time to shift, especially if you have been enjoying calling your boss an ass. Eventually it will become a habit, and not only make you a more relat*able* person; it will also support you becoming a more positive person overall.

THE LAST WORD . . .

Semantics are powerful. So often we are told "they're just words–they can't hurt you," but try asking someone to recall a time in which someone was cruel or unkind through words alone. You can be sure that they can remember the words, but also where they were and what they were wearing. Our words have the power to inspire, connect, and lead, and they also have the power to destroy. Choosing to be more empathetic, straightforward, and positive in your word choices will improve every conversation throughout your life.

LET'S DO THIS!

ACTION:

Who is a leader you admire? Listening to the words they say, how do they express themselves?

_____

_____

_____

How can you express yourself in a more empathetic way?

_____

_____

How can you express yourself more straightforwardly?

_____

_____

How can you express yourself more positively?

_____

_____

_____

MINDSET: I am aware of the words I say.

Chapter Nine

INSPIRE YOUR THEN WHAT?

Have you ever noticed that some people have extra sparkle? They stand a little taller and shine a little brighter. Their enthusiasm, passion, and confidence create a magnetism about them. You want to be where they are, buy what they sell, and listen when they speak because there is something very different about them.

For a moment, create a mental roster of the people that you "follow," not only on social media but particularly in real life. Those people are generally people that you find interesting, charming, and are naturally drawn to. Are there bosses you would work for regardless of the company they were with? Do you have a friend that you really admire? Maybe there's a colleague whom you find captivating? Now think about what draws you to them. I would bet that you're not enamored with the car they drive or their perfect selfie but rather something far more at the core of who they are.

You're drawn to their spark. They have a light so bright that it pulls you in like bugs to a zapper, minus the shock, death, and awful cleanup.

These individuals have a purpose that lights them up. A reason for jumping out of bed in the morning. An excitement for life and all it has to offer. They know their *then what.*

We can connect, communicate, and *then what*?

You get the job, and *then what*?

You make all these friends, and *then what*?

You create a network, and *then what*?

Our *then what* is the inner light that drives every interaction. You can absolutely ace connecting and communicating and still become relat*able* without it, but only when you find your inspiration, your *then what*, will you shine brighter and become even more magnetic and successful, because then people will see your heart.

WHERE IT ALL BEGAN

Twelve years ago, I was sitting on the couch with my then-husband when we started spitballing an idea. We had both always been inventive and entrepreneurial. He was always thinking of better ways to do things, from his teenage years when he tried to patent a heated steering wheel before they were common to drawing up plans for a kebab-making machine after we had divorced. I myself had been fascinated by business since the third grade. While other kids had lemonade stands, I had a full bakery and convenience store set up at the end of my parents' driveway, named Candy+ (because I sold candy and other things and was quite creative in my naming skills). My mom bought the inventory and baked all the cookies, while I kept all the profit. I was really on to something there.

It was a common couple's activity for us to come up with ideas, with the lawyer in me then crushing our dreams after a Google or patent search. This particular idea was interesting, though–it had legs. We started talking about how we met. He had passed a note to me through the waitress while I was having lunch with my parents. The gesture was sweet and bold, and it worked. It was also 2004. There were no dating apps, and though Match had been in existence for nearly nine years at that point, people were still hesitant about online dating, and they lied about where they met if they did meet on a site.

We talked about how often singles miss an opportunity to connect with someone they find attractive because they're afraid of rejection, or they're fearful of giving out their phone number to a rando. Stranger danger was still a thing–we weren't yet drunkenly jumping in random cars we ordered on an app. So archaic. The only shot those with a near-chance encounter had was Craigslist's "Missed Connections," where people would post in earnest, trying to find that person who caught their eye in the produce aisle or on the subway, but the likelihood of success was low. The two of us started brainstorming how we could create dating cards that would allow singles to avoid those missed connections. The buyer would get a deck of cards with fun and flirty sayings that they could pass out to anyone they found attractive, and if the feeling was mutual, they could connect online without exchanging personal information until they felt comfortable.

After running the idea past several trusted advisors (read: smart, successful people), we realized we had something with potential. We spent the next two years raising investment funds (over $1.3 million), creating the product and technological infrastructure, developing a launch plan, and applying for patents. It was exhilarating and exciting. I vividly recall being up at all hours of the night with my newborn, my rocking chair next to my iMac, working with one hand while she slept nestled in my other arm.

We launched with a bang. The concept landed us on the front page of the *New York Times* Style section, in the *Wall Street Journal*, and on almost all local TV networks in New York City. We even received a call from Oprah! Okay, her team called, and while that segment never came to fruition, I appeared on a multitude of media outlets representing the company. The more segments I did, the more they booked. The producers said I spoke well on camera and asked if I had opinions and advice about dating and flirting. Me, have opinions? Did I ever! I could get free hair and makeup at the studio, do a segment on a variety of dating topics, and plug the company. It was a win-win. The press coverage was phenomenal, but the sales were dismal. Actually, dismal is a generous term. Sales were nonexistent.

A year later, after a complete rebrand and relaunch due to that lack of sales, we were approached by a marketing guru affiliated with one of the sharks on *Shark Tank*. He loved the new look of the website and cards that were way cooler. We all believed that the concept was still relevant as there weren't yet apps taking over the market. We recognized that sales were nonexistent, but potential for growth was there. In order to save the business, he was convinced that I needed to become the face of the company and a "brand" in my own right. He was big into celebrity endorsement for selling power and believed that if I built my brand, my brand would lead to the company's success. He wanted me to become a "flirting expert"–his words and title, not mine!

At that point, I was a lawyer running a dating company. Actually, a start-up dating company with no sales and imminent risk of failure. All I could think was, "If I do this, there is no turning back." Juries would likely have questions about how I became involved in the dating industry. But becoming a *flirting expert*? Have you ever googled "flirting expert"? A quick scroll through the top search results easily proved that it was absolutely the end of my career as a trial attorney if this didn't work. It was also dangerous financially. We had spent all of the funds on development and marketing, and even without ever taking a salary over those years, we were still out of money. We started bootstrapping and borrowing, begging my mom to let us use her credit to open up a card since we were at our limits. In going down this path, not only would I lose my potential to slide back into law easily, but we'd be repaying debts for life. We did it anyway. I still thought it could work, and really, what option did we have? Quit? Not until we had to.

In spite of our efforts, the business failed. It was 2012 and the dating landscape changed seemingly overnight when a little company called Tinder came on the scene with the invention of the "swipe." All of a sudden, we were as antiquated as wooden wheels after the invention of tires. There was a new way to meet people with little effort, and no one wanted to be handing out cards that they had to purchase when they could simply load an app for free.

I was devastated and my life had collapsed. In addition to the company, our marriage also went down in flames. I was, at thirty-two, a former lawyer turned flirting expert, raising two kids on my own, and in need of a job.

Something weird had happened, though. I kept receiving requests for "coaching" from people who would see/hear/read my interviews. At the time, I had *zero* clue what coaching even was. The only coaching I was familiar with was in relation to sports, and as we know, I am not your girl for that. But I started talking to people. People in pain. People who were frustrated. People looking for guidance. People needing help.

So, I became a coach. I became a hypnotherapist. I studied human relationships (and continue to do so). I started working with people on everything from their flirting skills to their interpersonal relationships to their professional goals. We'd start out talking about flirting and dating and realize that it all ran far deeper than not knowing what to say to someone they were attracted to. My coaching was so much more than helping them date. I was helping them discover what was preventing their happiness and then helping them become happy.

And I became happy.

Of course, I would have loved to have made millions for myself and our investors in a tech start-up, and part of me will forever feel heartbroken over that failure. Yet that painful path led me to realize that my heart is filled through helping people.

In retrospect, I see my entire career path as a trajectory and an inter-woven web of experience. I became a lawyer to help create a little more fairness in the world, I became an entrepreneur to build connections, I became a coach to guide people through their challenges, and now I speak and write about relatability because connection is still what everyone craves.

I help people connect.

I know who I am. I know my purpose. I didn't always recognize it, and there have been hurdles along the way, but now? I own it and I show it. You can relate through connection and communication but to "inspire" takes everything to the next level.

We need to inspire people to connect with us and to want to stay con-nected. So let's think about your *then what*. Think, why are you really read-ing this book? What purpose does relatability serve in your life? What is your passion? Because the answers to those questions are your *then what*. Your *then what* is what drives you. It's what makes you shine.

WHAT IF I DON'T KNOW MY *THEN WHAT*?

You may be thinking, *I don't know what my* then what *is*. I was speaking at a conference for higher education professionals about the need to know and embrace your *then what*. While speaking, I recognized that there were several panicked faces in the crowd, so I paused and asked one woman whose face screamed alarm, "Why the look of terror?" She replied, "I have been on autopilot my entire life. I have *no* idea where to even start. I'm screwed."

No matter our age, we often spend much of our lives on autopilot. We pursue what we "should" do. We follow the leader aimlessly and don't rec-ognize it until we wake up five, ten, twenty years later wondering, *is this all there is?*

Take my client Luna. She was brilliant, beautiful inside and out and most notably, burnt out at twenty-six. She came to me amid a young midlife cri-sis (she was advanced in every way, so clearly everything happened earlier for her) and was about to drop out of medical school.

"I just can't do it. I'm miserable. I'm stressed all the time to the point that I can't sleep, and my hair is falling out," she relayed. Luna went on to explain that she was first generation in this country and her parents had placed enormous pressure on her to be successful in ways they felt they hadn't been able to be.

"Why do you think you're so stressed?" I asked.

"Because I have to be the best." Luna reminded me of another client, Michelle. (Remember the lawyer who couldn't handle being average among the most intelligent?) I was beginning to think I have a "type" of client.

"Do you even want to be a doctor?" By the heaving sigh in response, it was clear that she had dreaded this question and especially the requisite introspection that went with answering it. "I don't know, I used to think I did," she replied as her eyes began to well up.

I asked Luna to take some time to really think about why she decided to go to medical school and where things started to shift. I also asked that she write a letter to her younger self giving her advice on what she should do with her life. Two weeks later, I received a ping in my inbox with an attachment from Luna. The letter to her younger self.

Dear Luna,

I hope you are enjoying every minute of your sophomore year of college! What an amazing time to explore who and what you want to be?! Relish every moment with your friends and stop taking class so seriously–you'll get the A without the stress. And frankly, you can get a B or C and it's not going to be the end of the world–even if Dad thinks it is. I know they put a lot of pressure on you. It's so frustrating, but it's because they've never had an opportunity like this. They want the best for you, but they are also so blown away by how far you can go that they just want to keep pushing you up.

You need to be honest with them. You need to let them know that their pressure is doing more harm than good, and that you put enough pressure on yourself. You need to let them know they can love you without hurting you–even if it's not intentional.

You're going to have several opportunities for internships next year. Don't just take the most prestigious one. You hate labs and research. Even though you know Mom and Dad think you should be on the "find the cure for cancer" path, you know that is not your passion. Go work at the clinic. It's not going to give your parents as many bragging rights, but you will feel inspired every minute you get to interact with patients and see what medicine can do. If you take the lab job, you're going to be miserable. Trust me.

I wish I had been able to separate my passion from Mom and Dad's motivations at your age. I wish I had stood up for myself, lovingly, and let them know that my dreams for myself were just as good as theirs for me. Maybe I still can.

With love,
You. Or me. Us?
PS: Don't date Adam. He's an ass and you know it.

"I want to be a doctor. I just don't want to be the doctor they want me to be," Luna proclaimed at our first meeting after sending the letter. "I love what medicine can do. I want to be a healer. My parents expect me to find the cure for cancer, but I want to be helpful."

Luna knew her *then what* but she allowed external pressures to get in her way. She knew her *then what* but almost gave up the path to achieve it because she couldn't separate it from the *shoulds*. Our *shoulds* are what we (or others) think we *should* be doing. I *should* stop taking naps as an adult. My mom thinks I *should* write more. Luna thought she *should* value her parents' vision of her life over her own. Our *shoulds* don't always align with what we want to be doing or what feels right in our soul.

Luna and I spent some time talking through the changes that she needed to make, externally and internally, to reclaim ownership of her path. We created a plan for balance in her life as she finished medical school and started her residency. We talked through how she could lovingly and firmly create boundaries with her parents. Most of all, we worked on rewriting the script in her head to value her own aspirations above all and embrace her *then what* with every step.

Five years later, Luna is a physician at a children's clinic that supports underserved communities, and she couldn't be happier. Her parents may still wish that she had taken a more esteemed (read famous) path but learned to support her decision and are very proud. She will avoid waking up at fifty and realizing she was living someone else's dream.

HOW TO FIND YOUR *THEN WHAT*

Purpose is not what you find, it's what you create. It's what you choose. There are many paths to discovering what lights us up. My road to my purpose was winding (and expensive); Luna's were hidden under external influences, but they were always there. There was always a gut feeling that needed to be listened to, even if it is often ignored.

Take some time to think about what makes *you* happy. Not your parents. Not your friends. Not even your bank account. I have met very rich, very uninspired, and thereby very uninteresting humans in my life. I often walk away from those conversations wondering if they think money and material possessions is all there is to life. That's not to say that money isn't helpful or that being financially secure isn't an inspiration for some dreams. There are plenty of people in this world who place a high value on their finances, but my question would be, what drives that? Here are some questions that could help you start to percolate what inspires you:

- **What are you willing to work really hard for?** Your willingness to sacrifice, even if you don't actually have to, is the difference between something you accept because it's easy and available versus what you work for.
- **What type of person do you want to be?** Maybe you aren't ready to define what your life purpose is; maybe your *then what* is knowing the type of person you want to be.
- **What would your ten-year-old self say to you about your life and choices?** Our earlier versions are pretty wise. Ask You 1.0 for some feedback on You 5.0.
- **What scares you . . . in a good way?** There's a difference between my fear of spiders and my fear of failure. Life is about taking chances, and the bigger the chance, the scarier the leap.
- **Would you regret anything if you died tomorrow?** Morbid, I know, but helpful when looking at our true priorities.

It's important to note that your *then what* can change. I can hear you from here: *WHAT?! After all that introspection?!* But, yes, as we grow and evolve, our priorities and inspiration can change. Different times in your life can call for different versions of yourself. Luna may decide after twenty years at the clinic that her desire to help and heal could shift to needing more time with her family. There will be a series of events that happen on your journey where you'll have to say, what is my *then what?* Trust the journey.

THE LAST WORD . . .

It may seem odd to have an entire chapter in a book on relationship building to be focused on something as esoteric as finding your life's purpose. You may still be wondering how this elusive concept could possibly help diminish social anxieties and how you can integrate yours into what you're trying to achieve here, relatability. It's the secret weapon for all of it. People who know what really matters to them show up differently in every interaction. Someone who knows how they want to show up in this world stands a little taller. One who knows their *then what* shines brighter.

It's not that you need to talk about your purpose in every conversation; it's simply there, existing, and making you so much more magnetic.

LET'S DO THIS!

ACTION:

What is my *then what*? Is it who I am as a person or a definition of my purpose?

_____

_____

_____

How can I do more to nurture my *then what* in my life?

_____

_____

_____

MINDSET: My *then what* is _____, and it inspires every interaction.

PART THREE

The Who: How to Solve the
Most Common People Problems

Chapter Ten

TOO NICE
ISN'T SWEET

"I'm so sorry."

"Alexis, what are you apologizing for?"

"I've been rambling on, I don't think I'm making sense, and I feel like I'm complaining a lot."

"Uh, Alexis, you quite literally *pay* me to listen; you have complete control over what you want to talk about and how it comes out. I asked what happened on vacation, and you were answering."

"I know, but ugh, I just feel so whiny. I'm sorry."

"OMG, no more sorry!"

"Okay, sorry."

"Oh Alexis."

Alexis was a thirty-one-year-old new mom, new wife, and newly employed account manager at a midsize PR firm. Pretty much everything was new in her life, except for her very old and very ingrained trait of apologizing for things that weren't her fault. Even over the phone, I could tell she had another apology coming up quickly behind the last. As if she truly was sorry for not being the best possible client. Just like she had to be the best wife. The best mom. The best friend. The best employee. The best . . . everything.

Alexis was a certified people pleaser. We started working together because she was stressed and wanted to preserve her relationships, all of them—with her wife, her boss, and her son. She was so anxious that she had dropped ten pounds on her already small frame without trying, couldn't sleep, and started getting heart palpitations. Her stress was taking a very physical toll in addition to its psychological implications.

I recall asking her when we first connected, "So what brings you my way?" To which she replied, "Oh, I just want to be a better person." Even when she was stressed beyond belief, she was convinced that if only she was "better," then it would all get . . . better.

"Tell me about your typical day," I fished.

"Well, I wake up at 4:30 a.m. so I can be ready when my son gets up. He's eighteen months and an early riser, but I hate when he cries because he'll wake up Heather. She likes to sleep, so I wake up thirty minutes before he does and drink my coffee in the nursery."

"Do you like to sleep?" I asked. "Sure, but she has a way harder job and makes more money, so I want to make sure she gets as much rest as possible." All righty, self-sacrifice number one (of many). "Then I make everyone breakfast and get Braxton ready for day care, packing his bag and food for the day. I also like to make Heather a lunch because she prefers my sandwiches to anything she can find near her office. After that I drop Braxton off at day care around 8:30 a.m. and head to work."

"Does Heather ever offer to take part in the morning routine?" I replied, exhausted even thinking about Alexis's schedule before 9:00 a.m. "She does, but I don't let her. I want to do it, even though sometimes I resent how little she does. I know it doesn't make sense."

The rest of her average day played out in the same manner. She took on extra everywhere. At work she never took a lunch or even a moment to breathe, spending her day buried in her computer. Alexis believed that the more work she piled on, the more she would be valued. So her colleagues dumped even *more* on her.

At around 6:00 p.m. she would leave to pick up her son from day care, followed by dinner and Braxton bath duties. Heather got home at 7:30 p.m. with only enough time to put the baby to bed. "I feel terrible that I can't spend time with my wife at night but by 8:30 p.m., I'm exhausted and in bed myself. I'm too young to feel this old."

"What parts of your day are in your control? What can you change?"

"I don't know. If I changed anything, I feel like I would be disappointing people. Maybe I just need more coffee."

Coffee was not going to solve Alexis's problems. Her wife was frustrated. Heather appreciated all Alexis did, but didn't find her martyrdom attractive, and she actually wanted to take on more responsibility at home. Braxton wasn't getting any quality time with either parent, and while he was only eighteen months old at the moment, he would soon be both subconsciously *and* consciously aware of his moms' unhappiness. Alexis's boss was starting to question hiring her. He assumed that she must work at hyperspeed given all she asked to take on, until things started slipping. She missed a reporter's deadline. Her reports to clients were late and riddled with errors. Her job was on the line. "If you don't make changes, you won't have people around you to disappoint."

THE PERILS OF PEOPLE PLEASING

The desire to be liked can feel all-consuming. We make choices that we believe will increase our likeability and preserve our relationships, but those choices are at the expense of our own happiness and sanity. We say yes even though we feel a loud "no" resonating through our bodies. We feel underappreciated even though our own choices have led us to be taken advantage of. We are upset because we feel disrespected even when we don't respect ourselves.

Too nice is not too sweet. People pleasing, otherwise known as being a social conformist, can be dangerous at Alexis levels. There are differing degrees of conforming to fit in. Pretending to like your mother-in-law's cooking to preserve the relationship is very different than removing all of your opinions to avoid conflict or taking on every responsibility to prove your worth.

In terms of relatability, people pleasing just plain gets in the way. Those engaging with a people pleaser can lose respect, or worse, they can pity the pleaser because they know they can walk all over them. Anyone looking for balance in a relationship (like Alexis's wife) can become frustrated and angry with their inability to help and love equally. Those relationships are based on a falsity, and as we've learned, a false foundation will always crumble. The greatest value you can bring to any relationship is to show up as your truest strongest self.

ARE YOU A PEOPLE PLEASER?

I've met people who are clearly pleasers but didn't recognize the tendency within themselves. They knew they were unhappy and upset but couldn't pinpoint why. Below is not an exhaustive list, but if you can agree with a few of these signs, you may need to keep reading this chapter:

- You find it difficult to say no.
- You say yes but then regret it immediately.
- You often find yourself feeling unappreciated by those around you.
- You feel taken for granted by those you care about.
- You don't feel as if your partnerships are equal or balanced.
- You worry more about other people's feelings than your own.
- You apologize for everything, even breathing.
- You feel guilty when you don't want to do something.
- You want to be everything to everyone.

There comes a point where we have to stop being so nice and start being real. Real is where we create healthy sustainable relationships at work and at home. Real is how we know that the connections we are making are based on our true selves and not a fallacy.

There are three steps to stopping your people-pleasing ways:

1. **SET BOUNDARIES:** Boundaries protect our energy and demand respect. No is a complete sentence.
2. **TAKE A BEAT:** No more knee-jerk responses, because from this moment on, there is a moment of self-reflection before answering.
3. **PRACTICE ACCEPTANCE:** It's time to accept yourself and the fact that you can't make everyone happy. You aren't tacos.

SET BOUNDARIES

"I can't say no" is the statement I hear the most from those who aim to please. They take on too much, they allow people to take advantage of them, and they are afraid that if they say no or set a boundary, they won't be liked or loved. The problem is that in failing to say no, they won't be respected, either–by themselves or others. In many cases, people pleasers are taken advantage of because they *can* be.

I have a friend who is one of the sweetest people on earth. Eva would give you the last cent in her bank account if you needed it, even if her rent was due. She's there to support her friends, family, acquaintances, and even strangers on the street if they are having a bad day. She's kind and beautiful. Eva's also a devoted people pleaser. Her boss dumps work on her like a truck on a landfill and she takes it all on without question or comment. Her family is borderline abusive and manipulative, but she still bends over backward to help them in every way possible.

I often witness so-called friends taking advantage of her position and romantic interests benefiting from her codependency. Her lack of boundaries affects her health, happiness, and overall well-being. She sleeps terribly, gets sick often, and is filled with anxiety on a daily basis. She knows she needs to change, but nothing will if she doesn't stand up for herself and set some boundaries, starting with a solid "no" now and then.

Remember: No is a complete sentence. It requires no explanation. Even the most steadfast people pleasers recognize when something feels off. Eva will say things like, "I know I should say no" or "I immediately got (even more) anxious when they asked me to XYZ." There's a feeling in your gut when you know you have reached your limit. The challenge is to acknowledge it and then act on it.

Many pleasers have a hard time with a hard no, at least at first. If you prefer to ease into "no," try offering "no, but." For example: "Can you help me move this weekend?" Answer with something like, "No, but I know there are great people on Craigslist that can help you and definitely won't murder you!" Okay maybe not quite that, but you get the idea.

Alexis is a bit of a different scenario, as she wasn't being *asked* to take on extra responsibilities, she was freely heaping them on her plate! However, that doesn't mean that she didn't suffer from a boundary issue. In her case, Alexis needed to set a boundary around what was acceptable for her to handle and allow herself to give the rest away. Her boundary needed to be set around her intellectual, emotional, and physical limits. She needed to place as much of a value on herself as those around her. Alexis's "no" needed to be "no longer."

Creating boundaries allowed Alexis to unload responsibilities. We made a plan to present to Heather and then chatted a few weeks later. "I talked to Heather. I told her I couldn't do it all alone, even though I thought I could *and* thought I wanted to. It was weird, she was actually relieved! We made a split schedule where she gets up with Braxton on the weekdays and takes him to day care, and I do pickup, dinner, and bath time because her schedule still keeps her at work late."

"And how is that working for you two?" I asked. Alexis's voice was literally buzzing with excitement. "It's amazing. I'm so much more rested because I'm not waking up basically in the middle of the night. Heather gets extra time with Braxton, which she loves, and we are so much more connected because we feel like a team. I can't believe I avoided this for so long."

Once Alexis reclaimed balance at home, she turned to work. "I really messed this one up. Heather has to love me, right? My boss and colleagues don't. I feel like a failure. They'll probably fire me." Alexis didn't get fired, but after she talked to her boss about what was really going on, he was concerned that she wasn't able to assess her own limits. "He was already concerned with my work performance, so he put me on some sort of probation, and we are going to reevaluate things in ninety days. Thankfully he took some work off my plate, and I can really focus on doing a good job with what's in front of me." Alexis recognized that a level of damage was inflicted during her overwhelmed phase but feels confident that she can excel now that she had an appropriate workload. "I wish I had handled this sooner," she lamented later. "I didn't realize how dangerously close to drowning I was."

When we know better, we do better.

Alexis still struggles at times with her desire to make Heather's life easier. It makes sense—we should want to take care of those we love! The difference now is that she looks for balance in all she does. Whether you are struggling with "no" or "no longer," recognizing the power of setting boundaries is a good first step.

Boundaries protect our actions and our energy. In some cases, you may need to say "no" to an entire person. There are people who are simply toxic and should be boundaried out entirely, and we'll delve into that in the next chapter. Your happiness, sanity, and health are precious and should be treated as so.

Your physical and mental health are worthy of any boundary necessary to protect them. Try to imagine what your world would look like if you took the reins. How can you start to implement boundaries in your world? You are worthy of protection.

TAKE A BEAT

We humans are habitual creatures. I get up and brush my teeth every morning, still half-comatose. I then head downstairs, throw a mug under my Nespresso machine (I'm addicted), and give the dog water and food. Every morning. Regardless of what state I'm in. It's subconscious. Similarly, many people pleasers say yes without thinking.

If you've been a certified pleaser for some time, we have a habit to break. You're probably naturally inclined to accept as opposed to question someone's request. In order to break that habit, we have to take a beat and use that pause to ask ourselves, "Am I saying yes to this because I want to, or because I think I should?" Anytime that you are asked to do something, give yourself a second to make a gut check. Prior to asking for more responsibility at work, take a second. A simple reflective "why?" can make a huge impact.

I asked my friend Eva to try pressing pause before acquiescing. "It's hard. I'm so used to just saying yes and then dealing with the regret," she shared after a week of practicing the take-a-beat approach. "But I took a breath after my boss came in and asked me to take on another project. I actually let him know my workload was already overwhelming, but if it wasn't a priority, I could handle it when things calm down. I think he was a bit taken aback, but he ended up telling me to just focus on what I had in front of me! It was weird, and awesome."

Saying yes without thinking became a habit after doing so repeatedly; similarly, taking a beat before answering needs consistent practice to become second nature. If you feel you have to say something, "maybe" or "let me think about it" or "I'll get back to you" is a great delay. There is no harm in taking a moment before anyone asks anything of you so you can assess the situation and make a decision that feels good, because you know what happens to your gut and anxiety levels when it doesn't.

PRACTICE ACCEPTANCE

Acceptance is twofold. We need to accept our limitations and accept the discomfort that will come when shifting out of people-pleasing ways.

"I really wish I could have handled it all." After a few months of some serious life shifts, Alexis was still struggling with her own acceptance challenges. I assured her that it was completely normal to feel this way. "It's important that you recognize you couldn't handle it all, and no one could have! You tried to take on a herculean effort, and it was unsustainable."

We are mere humans. At least I am. There is a limit to what we can handle emotionally and physically. When I go to the gym, I know I can't deadlift three hundred pounds or run a five-minute mile. I could try, but I'd probably kill myself or at least end up in traction. I push myself to my limits, but I stop there. I wish it was that way with people pleasing. Somehow when it comes to taking care of others, we can become blind to our limitations. We take on more and more until we are collapsing under the weight of responsibility. Acceptance means "I know and accept my limits, and that's okay."

It can be difficult to recognize that we have a maximum capacity, but vital for people-pleasing recovery. Repeat after me:

I know and accept my limits, and that's okay.

I know and accept my limits, and that's okay.

I know and accept my limits, and that's okay.

It's equally necessary to accept that there will be discomfort along the way. There will be people who don't react kindly to your new strength, and why would they? They reaped the benefits of taking advantage of the situation. Accept that it's going to be uncomfortable at times. Accept that things can become contentious. Accept that not everyone will like you. Accept that you *are* important.

Acceptance is a practice, both of yourself and the situation. It will get easier with time and practice, but please be gentle with yourself during the process.

THE LAST WORD . . .

People pleasing seems innocuous until you break down the effects, not only on the pleaser, but on their relationships. The habit can lead to dangerous levels of stress and anxiety, and while I'm sure you are super powerful, we all have limits. Set boundaries, take a beat, and practice acceptance and your people-pleasing ways will shift with consistent effort. In addition to the steps in this chapter, I'd also encourage a reread of Chapters Three and Four, which focus on authenticity and confidence. Both can boost what you may need to stand in your power and put yourself first.

LET'S DO THIS!

ACTION:

Are there relationships in your life that could use better boundaries? What limits can you create to protect yourself?

_____

_____

_____

How can you better prioritize yourself throughout your day?

_____

_____

_____

What will you need to accept in order to shift any people-pleasing ways?

_____

_____

_____

MINDSET: I know and accept my limits, and I will set boundaries to protect them.

Chapter Eleven

IT'S NOT YOU, IT'S THEM

Relationships are our greatest teachers; they help us grow and evolve. They make us better people if we let them and provide a level of fulfillment to our lives. Unless they don't. Most relationships are meant to be, but not every relationship is meant to be forever. Whether professionally, personally, or romantically, there can be expiration dates attached to our connections, some dates coming earlier than others. And in certain cases, you should avoid that relationship entirely.

There are people in this world that you are simply not meant to connect with or stay connected to. There are connections that not only fail to lift you up but actively bring you down and people that suck the life out of every conversation. Those that try to make you feel less than or unimportant. Toxic relationships where the only choice is choosing "you" and walking away, and trust me, it's not you, it's them.

BEEN THERE, DONE THAT

He bought a new Mercedes E-Class for our first date.

I can't even recall what he was driving before that, but apparently it seemed like an ideal time to level up. I was a twenty-five-year-old law student and single mom of a four-year-old, living at my parents' house, while he was a twenty-seven-year-old financial advisor and single dad of a seven-year-old. We met in a very unconventional way (that led to the creation of our company, as I talked about in Chapter Nine) after he passed a note through the waitress as I lunched with my parents. It seemed like kismet after our first conversation. Two go-getter single parents who loved their children and career path but were lonely.

We went to all the best restaurants. Within a week of dating, he up-graded my cell phone to the newest model. The following week he bought me a purse I'd been fawning over for a year but couldn't swing (nor justify). Every week he brought me a fresh dozen roses to keep in my room. We integrated into each other's daily lives quickly, and before I knew it, either he was at my parents' house for dinner nightly or I was out with him. He couldn't let twenty-four hours go without seeing me. If I hurt, he hurt. If I was stressed, he was stressed. His world seemed to revolve around me, and I ate it up.

We were engaged in six weeks. I guess I shouldn't be surprised. I mean, he told me he loved me on our third date. All of this seems insane to me now, but to twenty-five-year-old Rachel, who had low self-esteem and was broke, raising a kid, and dying to move out of her parents' house, it was heaven. After all, he essentially worshipped the ground I walked on. We never fought. Our kids got along great. What could go wrong?

Ten months after we met, we were married. We spent our honeymoon moving into a beautiful new house, and I felt as if I were on top of the world.

Until I wasn't.

It took two months into our marriage to see a completely different side of him. The one that yelled at me for no reason, that called me horrible names, and taunted my emotions when I reacted. I'd be lying if I said I was completely blindsided. There was, after all, a temper I had seen in the past, along with a good amount of jealousy. Like the time he insisted on a joint bachelor/bachelorette party in Atlantic City, so he could make sure I behaved. The one that he canceled mid-party because a random guy was hitting on me and he could see it from across the casino. The "party" that sent my best friend home crying because she was afraid for me.

I thought he was overprotective. That he loved me so much that he couldn't bear to imagine losing me to someone else. That he was fiery and passionate. Not that he was controlling. Or emotionally abusive.

I spent seven years in that marriage. What can I say. I'm committed! Or should have been committed. Things got worse, way worse, before they got better. The union was riddled with addiction and mental illness and anger and sadness. It was excruciatingly painful, and I was far more lonely than I was before meeting him. There was a public face and a private face on our marriage, and no one had a clue of how terrible things truly were.

In fairness to him and our union, there *were* some good times. We loved our kids fiercely, he adopted my son on all but paper, and together we created a beautiful daughter and a company that led me here. We had a lot of . . . things. I wanted for nothing and had more purses and diamonds than anyone would need, many as tokens of apology for losing thousands in Atlantic City or getting drunk in the middle of the day . . . again. So yes, while there was good, it was irreparably toxic. I tried to force therapy/rehab/interventions, yet nothing stuck. I recall being in counseling trying to sort through all of my sadness and frustration, telling my therapist I found the book title that summed it all up, *Too Good to Leave, Too Bad to Stay*. She responded by handing me a copy of *Codependent No More*. I got the hint. I left.

If I looked back with the maturity and self-worth that I now have, I would have done things differently. However, I regret nothing. My daughter's existence is worth it all. My current relationship with the love of my life is worth all of the knowledge I gained ever so painfully. Even so, I would not wish the path I chose on anyone. My life lessons were expensive in terms of emotional currency.

Red flags are real, and we need to stop ignoring them. Toxic relationships will kill your spirit if you don't walk away from them. You are worthy of happiness and peace.

I used to joke during a speech that humans could rationalize anything and anyone if they were attractive enough. "Sure, he murdered twenty people, but how cute is he?! Did you see his biceps? Probably from hacking all those bodies, but swoooooon!" Our common sense can become questionable when we want something badly enough, be it a relationship, a job, a friend.

James was as adept at ignoring red flags, too. He was always interested in making money. From the age of seven, he would tell his mom weekly that he was going to be a millionaire. She'd smile and nod as she looked around their modest one-bedroom apartment, wondering if she let him watch too much TV. As if vision boarding were an elementary school class, by nine, he had a picture of a Ferrari, mansion, and private plane on his wall along with words like *loaded*, *money*, and *bling*. To no one's surprise, when he graduated from college with a degree in finance, he headed straight to Wall Street. A professor connected him with a hiring hedge fund, with the warning, "Be careful what you wish for." James scoffed at the idea that there was anything or anyone he couldn't handle in the name of making money.

The interview for his peon-level position was over Skype with a senior-level employee who seemed somewhat normal, though distracted, which James attributed to the interviewer being on a business trip in California at the time. He was hired on the spot thanks to his killer GPA, references, and clear ambition. The moment he walked into the office on his first day, he was almost euphoric. He could smell the Italian leather in his soon-to-be new Ferrari. He knew it was time to hustle. James was prepared to do whatever it took to reach the goals he set in childhood and never wavered from. He took a deep breath and smiled, feeling on top of the world. For a moment, at least.

"James. My office. Now. This is not a fucking vacation. Stop sleeping on the job, you lazy shit!" his new boss shouted at him before he could even take off his jacket. He'd heard stories about Steve. Reddit and Glassdoor had had a field day with this guy. He was notorious, but nothing James couldn't manage, right? "I don't care what you thought was going to happen here. I actually don't care about you at all," Steve snarled as he threw a stack of research at him, along with his dry-cleaning tickets. "You're temporary. You get no breaks. No vacation. No sick days. Don't get sick. Don't sleep. Just show up and shut up, and remember, you're my bitch."

That first week alone James spent more time watching people do cocaine off office desks than he did sleeping in his bed. He declined to partake, to which his colleagues replied with a laugh and "just wait." Steve took turns berating the staff, seemingly on rotation and without reason, and with a special place for James. He was anticipating a long workday, but eighteen hours every day was not in the brochure. Colleagues didn't even bother going home half the time. They instead napped at their desk in twenty-minute increments. No wonder they needed stimulants. James thought if he only proved himself and showed Steve how essential he could be, then his boss would change. He thought that maybe he was trying to motivate the team in a way the self-help section books had overlooked. He was in denial that Steve was abusive and that his abuse was wrecking him.

By month four, James was on a permanent caffeine drip and had convinced his doctor he had ADHD to get a prescription for Adderall. The euphoria of his first moment in the office turned to dread every time he went through the swirling doors in the morning. His heart was doing weird things, but he was too busy and too terrified of taking time off to get checked out. He started to flinch every time Steve yelled; he'd brace for impact. More than once he found himself ready to cry in the bathroom. He was anxious, depressed, and living in terror at twenty-two.

Toxic relationships don't all look the same. They can take many forms.

It can be as dramatic as the workplace relationship James endured, or slightly less extreme but still impactful, as the colleague who constantly undermines your work or the boss who belittles every idea you have and then steals them.

Toxic relationships look like the friend who takes and takes and takes but never gives. Or the friend who spreads rumors and pretends it wasn't them to your face. They look like my first marriage, or that relationship you had that you knew made you feel bad, though you may not have recognized why.

WHAT ARE RED FLAGS?

There are always glaringly obvious "run!" signals like abuse, but oftentimes the behaviors we need to look out for in toxic relationships are more subtle and nuanced. They're actions that maybe you could justify at first, but after they accumulate, you recognize they're simply not right. Notably, not every red flag applies to every type of relationship. James's boss didn't tell him what to wear, but he was controlling in other ways, like dictating who he was allowed to associate with in the industry. Let's walk through some red flags (note, this is *far* from an exhaustive list) to help identify when a relationship may need further inspection before further interaction.

- **THEY CONSTANTLY CRITICIZE OR BELITTLE YOU.** You can do no right, even when you know you've done something well. They are far more interested in keeping you small than praising your accomplishments.
- **IT'S ALWAYS ALL ABOUT THEM.** Always. There is no room for you in their life or your conversations. They are so "me" focused that you leave wondering if they know a thing about you, even if you've known them for years.

- **THEY TRY TO CONTROL YOU.** They make all the decisions, like who you spend time with, what you do, what you wear. Your autonomy is irrelevant.
- **THEY WON'T COMMUNICATE WITH YOU AND DISREGARD YOUR EMOTIONS**. If they could run right over your thoughts and feelings, they would. There is no "talking things through," there is only how they feel and your silence.
- **THEY IGNORE YOUR BOUNDARIES, BOTH PHYSICAL OR EMOTIONAL.** You ask them to stop an action, and they don't. You tell them something bothers you, and they continue to do exactly that.
- **THEY BLAME EVERYTHING ON YOU.** They take no responsibility for mishaps, and everything is your fault, all the time.
- **THEY DON'T TRUST YOU, AND IT'S WITHOUT REASON.** There are times where trust issues are warranted, but you've done nothing wrong, and they make you feel like you did. All the time.
- **YOU FIND YOURSELF JUSTIFYING THEIR ACTIONS OR WORDS TO YOURSELF OR OTHERS.** They do or say something that you know is wrong, but you defend them to your friends, colleagues, and loved ones.
- **EVERYONE AROUND YOU SAYS, "ARE YOU SURE?"** One person's opinion is just that, an opinion. Gather three or more of the same opinions, and it's likely a fact. Listen to those who care about you, especially when they're in unison.
- **YOUR GUT TELLS YOU SOMETHING IS WRONG.** They may not have hit a single flag on this list, but if your gut tells you something is off, it's important to listen. We know how we feel after interacting with someone, and if it feels wrong it probably is wrong.

In many situations, these flags run in packs like wolves. They piggyback on one another until you can't help but see how awful this relationship is for your psyche. It's important that we look at the relationships in our life with eyes wide open. No one gets a pass, even those who can help you buy a Ferrari one day.

CHOOSE YOU

James's mom was the one who reached out to me. She had seen me talk about self-care on a morning show and was extremely worried about what was happening to her son. He had come home for Easter after nine months on the job and was a shell of the boy she raised and sent out into the world. Over dinner she described his sunken eyes with dark circles and his irritability toward everyone in the family. She recalled that while everyone was dying to talk to him about his big-time Wall Street job, he would only snap and shut them down in reply. I told her I would talk to him if he was open to it, and after she begged him for weeks, he finally relented.

"I'm fine. My mom just worries a lot," he started our initial call with.

"I get that. I'm a mom, too. I worry all the time, but why don't you tell me what's going on," I replied. After assuring him that I wouldn't share anything with his mom without permission, James proceeded to spill it all. The verbal abuse from his boss. The drugs. The insanity of his workload and oh yeah, that time Steve threatened to kill him if the stock he suggested tanked. James thought he was kidding, but honestly? He wasn't sure.

"You realize this is a toxic relationship, right?"

"Um, I'm not in a relationship with my boss."

"Well, yes, you are. Just as we are in relationships with our friends, family, and colleagues. Relationships are just a connection to another person, and this one is a problem."

"I can't quit. I have goals. There are guys that have been there forever, I can do this."

James started to sound like me when I didn't initially want to leave my marriage. I was committed. I made a commitment. My level of responsibility has always been high, and it felt wrong to walk away until I realized the impact it was having on me and my children.

"You can't reach your goals if you don't live long enough to achieve them," I responded.

He knew that he wasn't only burning the candle at both ends, he was throwing the whole thing in an incinerator. It took another several months of coaching before James felt strong enough to walk away, but walk away he did. A year later, the light behind his eyes was back and he had found a job as an analyst that may not make him a millionaire by twenty-three, but will get him his Ferrari one day, even if it's certified pre-owned.

It's hard to walk away from certain situations, especially when you're deeply entrenched. It's easy to make excuses or try to rationalize, until it isn't. Sometimes we are able to spot a toxic relationship at the outset and avoid it all together, but other times we have to be strong enough to choose ourselves.

You are worthy of being in a healthier situation. Your health and well-being are important. You are important. If it feels off, if the red flags are there, if you're being negatively impacted, it's time to choose you.

THE LAST WORD . . .

It's not always easy, but it's worth it. Leaving my marriage with two young children and no stable income as an entrepreneur was terrifying. There was so much to lose, and so many unknowns, but leaving was the best decision I ever made. My world became infinitely more peaceful, and my children happier. It even improved my relationship with my ex-husband (most of the time), as the only thing to focus on became our children. There are many who may look at my situation or James's and say, "Stick it out!" To which I reply, "At what expense?"

We have one life. Why would we live it in a way that hurts us? Choose you.

LET'S DO THIS!

ACTION:

Are there currently toxic relationships in your life? With whom? How are they affecting you?

_____
_____
_____

What are the red flags you see?

_____
_____
_____

How can you eliminate toxic relationships from your life?

_____
_____
_____

MINDSET: I choose me.

Chapter Twelve

THE CRITICAL SMILE

I've never met someone masochistic enough to actually enjoy being criticized. While constructive criticism is necessary, especially in a workplace setting, it's often perceived negatively by the recipient. We can take criticism personally, feeling judged and becoming defensive. Any helpfulness of the critique can be lost to emotion, and the criticism fails to land in a beneficial way.

At some point in your life, you will be asked to provide critical feedback to someone. It could be a friend, colleague, team member, or a loved one. As criticism is clearly a field filled with possible land mines, following a formula to protect your relatability is crucial. The goal is to preserve the relationship after giving feedback and this is why I created the Critical Smile. It's a way to be honest while maintaining the connection.

This Critical Smile is not to be confused with the compliment sandwich, which sandwiches criticism between two compliments. An example of a compliment sandwich would be, "Megan, you have been working so hard! I see you here past six every night. Though, your reports have had a lot of errors in them. Many have been unusable. But I really appreciate your dedication to the team."

Uh, what? Did I do something right or wrong? Am I valuable or not? Is my job secure? Megan is left with more questions than answers. Further, we're wired to focus on the beginning and end messages, and the middle statement gets ignored like a middle child. Megan may not even have taken in the critique of her work. Eat the compliment sandwich with your Critical Smile.

The Critical Smile is different and far more effective. It involves a four-pronged approach:

1. Start with the main point.
2. Get into the "teeth" of the matter.
3. End with a goal.
4. Do it all with kindness.

1. START WITH THE MAIN POINT

We need to set the stage for conversation by not trying to hide the main point. Beginning with a clear indication of what the conversation is about is essential to creating an atmosphere of respect. Where the compliment sandwich can feel insincere by starting with a compliment and then criticizing, starting with the main point allows the recipient to prepare themselves for having a possibly difficult conversation. This isn't a bad thing! Difficult conversations are inevitable in life, but if we enter into them with eyes wide open, we can engage more productively.

Isabella was still trying on the role of "boss" when her team at the marketing firm she had worked at for five years grew from two to six after taking on a new client. Half of her crew were older than her, the other half way cooler, and Isabella was convinced she would never be respected. Her first meeting with the team was disastrous. The client had given a very specific direction for their materials, and Isabella couldn't have been clearer when passing the requirements on to the copywriter and designer. The problem was that what she received was undeliverable. The graphics were amateur. The copy was dull. Isabella called a meeting with the responsible parties.

"So, uh, you guys are really great. You know I trust your instincts and talent. I'd love to know what your thoughts were in designing and writing this piece."

The designer and writer went on to share their process.

"Got it. Okay, well it's just that, well, it's not what the client is looking for. It's good and all, but we have to start over."

Uh. You could have led with that Isabella. Now you have two employees who a) thought they were being praised for their work, b) thought you were saying it was good (when it wasn't), and c) are now completely frustrated and somewhat embarrassed after detailing why they did what they did.

What would have worked better? A simple, "Hey guys, this work misses the mark of what the client is looking for. Let's go through the requirements again and their mission." It's not insulting. It's not harsh. It's honest and accurate. That statement would have enabled Isabella to lead into the next section of the Critical Smile with her team in a way that prepared them to dive into what needed to change.

Here are some ways you can start a critical conversation with clarity in professional and personal settings:

- It seems you may be taking on too much; let's talk about your workload.
- Let's discuss what's getting in the way of your punctuality.
- Your contributions are awesome, but we need to talk about how they are presented.
- Why don't we look at your time management process?
- I think we need to divide up household responsibility more evenly.
- It would be great if we talked more/spent more time together.
- I've noticed you've been less engaged lately; can we talk about why?
- It's difficult to have a discussion when I feel interrupted.
- It feels like you've been really negative lately; can we talk about it?

In each of the above statements or questions, it's possible to imagine the scenario that would lead to a need to give constructive criticism. There are limitless scenarios, from an employee or colleague whose performance is below par, to a romantic partner who isn't showing up in your relationship in the way you need them, to a friend who can't stop complaining. In all cases, leading with a broad stroke of what is to come is not only respectful, it's most productive.

2. GET INTO THE "TEETH" OF THE MATTER

A smile is as good as its teeth, and a critique is only as good as what surrounds it. The problem with most critiques is that they are served without context. Many times, the critiquer has reached a point of frustration and simply wants to unburden themselves. They aren't thinking about how this issue can be talked through. But talking through the context of a criticism is a vital component.

An especially important component of the discussion is to include more positivity than negativity in the teeth of the matter. Research has shown that ratios of positive to negative interactions are important predictors in the success of relationships, and these are all relationships that we want to preserve! The best predictor of a stable marriage is the ratio of positive to negative exchanges. If there are more negative encounters than positive, divorce is likely.[1] The same premise can apply in the workplace, with the highest-performing teams using a higher proportion of positive to negative comments.[2] Evidence has shown that positive emotions allow us to take in more of the surrounding contextual information.[3]

What does a positively weighted conversation about context look like? Let's go back to Isabella. After recognizing that her first attempt at critical feedback was a bust, Isabella reached out after reading a post I wrote on criticism. We talked through what the relationships looked like between her and the team at this moment, and while she knew they had lost some of their mojo together, they could recover. "I know I'm going to have to do this again, and I don't want to mess it up this time." She had that opportunity only a week later when the team's web designer showed her a site that didn't include the functionality requested by the client.

"Hey Max, we need to look at the flow here. We're missing some key elements," she began. Max, who was now bought in, continued to listen. "Your use of white space is brilliant, and I really love the way you're mixing images and copy to engage. I know you know how to make this site beautiful, but we still need to add in the functions the client asked for. Let's go through those specifically and see where they fit."

Max felt validated in his abilities, but still recognized that he had to make changes. Isabella's use of positive feedback allowed Max to remain engaged in the conversation while being more receptive toward understanding elements that were incorrect.

In all of our constructive criticisms, we need to talk through the context. Why is this a problem? What have you observed? Explain your position but do so in a way that allows the recipient to take in that information with a positively weighted discussion.

This works in personal relationships as well. For example, if you need to have a talk with your partner about a lack of communication, you could lead with something like, "I've been feeling like we aren't communicating as well lately." After laying the foundation, you can point out positive things in your relationship and include why you believe that communication is lacking. It could look like, "I love you; I think you are the kindest human on the planet, and I love our time together. It's just our communication; it feels like we just aren't on the same page we used to be. I really needed to talk after that fight last week, and you wouldn't. You are so important to me; I don't want this to get in the way of us."

In any situation, they have to understand where we are coming from. We have to be willing to explain what led to needing to give this criticism and have this conversation. They will take it all in much more effectively if you can find a way to incorporate positive elements.

3. END WITH A GOAL

The recency effect indicates that we remember the end of the conversation the most, which is why we always need to end with a goal. Like the end of a smile, the goal is heading up! It's indicating how to resolve the problem and avoid it reoccurring.

Isabella did just that with Max. After reviewing what content needed to be incorporated in order to meet the client's objectives, she ended with, "Okay, great. I know you can make all this happen pretty quickly, and that we won't have to talk about this kind of stuff again. I'm going to need a revision by next week with everything we talked about; does that work?" Max agreed and delivered the work ahead of schedule. He gave extra attention to client requirements from that moment on.

Goals can be set in all situations. That couple having a conversation about communication? Their goal could be to agree to talk out a fight within twenty-four hours, giving time for a cooling-off period, if necessary. If a colleague needed to be talked to about their time management challenges, the goal could include setting new deadlines and creating a plan to meet them. If a friend was being unnecessarily negative, the goal could be to become more aware of their pessimism.

The goal doesn't have to be some sort of extraordinary statement; it simply needs to accomplish sending the conversation in a direction that resolves the issue. We can criticize, but without resolution, all we're doing is complaining ourselves.

4. DO IT ALL WITH KINDNESS

As an expert in the media, I'm often asked to give my opinion on situations, people, and relationships. From the couples on *Married at First Sight* to Kate Gosselin on *Kate+Date* to the latest celebrity news, I've given my thoughts on a *lot* of people and their relationships. I had a memorable appearance on the *Tamron Hall Show* where her team invited me on to discuss a new TLC show, *I Love a Mama's Boy*, and to address with the cast some of the challenges of being in a relationship with a mama's boy. The producers sent over footage from the show, and my jaw dropped at the antics of these moms, the pure dysfunction of the relationship, and the death sentence it gave to any healthy romantic relationship these guys could try to have.

During my appearance, I made it clear that these were codependent and unhealthy relationships, but I didn't attack the moms. And people were surprised. I received so many messages and feedback from loved ones saying things like "You should have told them how insane they were!" or "I can't believe you were so respectful to those nut jobs!" Trust me, I agreed that these moms had some issues to be tackled and preferably by a professional. You don't go on a couple's cruise with your adult son, track his car, or guilt him into putting you first without having emotional or psychological challenges to work through. In theory, I would have been justified in leading with, "You all are nuts and are committing emotional incest," but can you imagine the reaction to that? The moms would get angry. The sons would get defensive. They all would tune out.

I could lead with aggression or an attack, but to what end? I'm not interested in being entertainment; I want to be education. My goal on TV is to use the exposure as a teaching moment. My hope is that someone somewhere listens and hears information that they can use in their lives, and it would be an even greater win if the subject of my thoughts—in this case, the moms and their sons—took something away from my words. The only way that will happen is if I can criticize while being kind.

I believe that kindness, especially during criticism, is the secret sauce. You may be thinking, *Wait, I told them positive things. Isn't that enough?* You can tell someone something positive without being kind. You can say, "You do a great job" with a touch of anger. Adding kindness to the mix is all about the intent and empathy.

How would you want criticism to be delivered? What tone would be most helpful in creating a change of behavior? When we place ourselves in the shoes of the recipient of the critique, it's easier to see how important kindness in delivery is.

You may not be prepping to give your opinion of someone's relationship on TV, but we are all critics at some point. In many situations, we are called upon to provide honest feedback and constructive criticism—as leaders, as friends, and as colleagues. However, the delivery can leave the recipient hurt, frustrated, angry, and confused. We can do it all with kindness.

THE LAST WORD . . .

Criticism is unavoidable, as the giver and the receiver. However, with the Critical Smile, it's far more palatable and far easier to provide—even if it requires a bit more intention on your part. Give the recipient the respect of starting with the truth of why you're having this conversation, discuss why it's important and include positive elements, end with a goal that resolves the challenge, and remember to be kind throughout. The Critical Smile will transform your most difficult conversations.

LET'S DO THIS!

ACTION:

How have you delivered criticism in the past?

_____

_____

_____

Thinking of a difficult conversation you may need to have, how can you use the Critical Smile to rewrite the script?

_____

_____

_____

MINDSET: I will rethink my critiques.

Chapter Thirteen

SMIZING IS REAL

Oh, 2020. What did we do to deserve you? Quite literally overnight, the way we lived our lives and interacted with others completely changed. We were thrown into a new way of working, communicating, and teaching. I am sure that I'm not alone in saying that I seriously missed hugs. In some ways, it made everything we've been discussing to this point so undeniably important. We need connection. We need relationships. We need contact.

Covid-19 also resulted in a serious pivot in all aspects of society (sorry, I couldn't help myself!), and we have shown our flexibility in so many areas with a shift to virtual . . . everything. We are now familiar with virtual meetings, court, conferences, school, dates, happy hours, family reunions, and holiday dinners. Between 2019 and 2020, Zoom grew from having just 10 million to seeing over 300 million daily meeting participants. No wonder Zoom fatigue is a real thing. Many had to learn a completely different skill set, and others are still trying to figure out how to turn their camera on and microphone off.

The in-person exchanges that we are having are also markedly different, or I should say "maskedly" different. Masks are required in many situations throughout the country, with no end date in sight, and they pose their own challenges to building relationships. Many in Asia have been covering up their faces in public for decades, with the deadly outbreak of SARS and air pollution inspiring many to mask up. However, in America, it was rare to see someone in a mask unless you were on a packed flight during flu season. That has changed for a large majority of the population, and we are now donning masks in schools, stores, shopping, at work, and anywhere you're not hanging solo. Regardless of your personal take on the effectiveness of masks, they have undoubtably created hurdles to overcome in terms of connection. The primary challenge being that when we are covering half our face, many of the non-verbal cues in conversation are eroded. We have a harder time reading emotions and smiles are hidden. The only people winning are those with resting bitch face.

How do we show up virtually in a way that is authentic and effective?

How do we stay connected when we are apart?

How can we show emotions and connect as powerfully as when our pearly whites are on display?

We can do all of this and more! I feel like I'm on an infomercial and about to throw in a pack of Ginsu knives, but really, there is a way to thrive in this new world. And yes, smizing is real.

VIRTUALLY VERSATILE

There are many elements of this new world that will likely return to some version of normal at some point; however, I would bet everything I own that virtual connecting is here to stay. Workplaces will take advantage of lowered overhead and sustained production by allowing employees to continue to work remotely. Workplace-related travel will likely see a change as well, with executives recognizing the cost effectiveness of an hour-long video meeting compared to thousands spent in airfare and accommodations. Virtual will also likely extend far beyond the workplace, with daters continuing to vet their matches via video before meeting IRL and families with loved ones interspersed throughout the world continuing to connect via camera.

If video is here to stay, why not hack the system to show up as your best self in every virtual setting? I've outlined three ways to stay virtually versatile and be relatable on camera:

1. BE ENERGY EFFICIENT: Avoid exhaustion and have enthusiasm.
2. GO INTO HIDING: Yes, you're gorgeous, but stop staring.
3. CHECK YOURSELF: Put your best torso forward every time.

1. BE ENERGY EFFICIENT

Have you ever noticed how much energy it takes to appear virtually as compared to in real-life situations? As a keynoter, I've always felt the rush of adrenaline before and during a speech and the subsequent dip when I'm ready to go hide in my hotel room and order room service. The aftershock of a virtual event is incomparable.

I recently delivered a virtual keynote followed by a workshop to a college organization. It was only two hours of talking, and if you've read this far, you can probably gather that I have no problem yapping away. It shouldn't be hard at all, right? Especially considering I could do the entire gig in yoga pants and slippers. I delivered the keynote and then chugged coffee during the five minutes I had in between the sessions. Once the workshop wrapped, I could barely walk from my office to the living room, collapsing on my couch, only waking to the poking finger of my daughter wondering when I was going to feed her dinner.

I was wiped in a way I have never experienced before.

When you're speaking or meeting in person, there is a give-and-take of energy. You are able to make eye contact and tell when people are invested and listening. Their smiles and nods are affirming and uplifting. You can also easily spot those not paying attention and give them a guilt-induced stare-down. Equally exciting. In a virtual setting, that reciprocal effect is suppressed. You give, but you don't get. It's utterly exhausting, without any of that infusion of energy.

Another reason our energy is depleted is how much harder our brains have to work. On video, our cognitive workload (mental effort related to what you're doing) is on overdrive.[1] We are simultaneously trying to figure out who's talking, doing our best to avoid talking over one another (with zero nonverbal cues), and determining what to say that makes us sound the best. And all the while we have to view ourselves, leading to extra anxiety for many. We're trying to pay attention to so many things at once, and our brains are paying the price.

If you are involved in any way in a virtual engagement, you have to conserve your energy (clearly this doesn't apply to the camera-off, muted, Instagram-scrolling participant we all dream to be). You can protect your energy by choosing where to focus and how to prep. If you are like most of us and feel the drain of seeing a sea of virtual faces, minimize that drain by minimizing the window. If I am doing a keynote, I avoid looking at anyone by blocking everything except the camera with a piece of paper taped to the screen. It's so unlike my tactic at in-person events where I live for eye contact, but I am aware of my ability to get thrown off when I see someone twirling in their chair or doing squats (it's happened). My focus on only the camera results in a better delivery for my client and allows my brain to close a few tabs. In more interactive conversations, I focus only on the person talking, using speaker view and sticky notes to cover up other aspects of the screen. It's low tech but efficient in reducing distraction and preventing energy drain.

Your prep on the day of the event matters as well. The prep involved is dependent on the importance and length of the event. If you know you have to be present in a significant way, plan your time around your meeting. Get rest, get caffeinated, and avoid all other activities that drain you. I now have a ritual on days I speak virtually: I avoid the gym in the morning (I don't get people who get energized by a morning workout!), I avoid alcohol the night before, and I have a cup of coffee thirty minutes before I start. I also make sure to give myself the grace to collapse afterward.

As in many areas of life, we can only control so much. So let's control what we can: our approach to appearing virtually, our awareness of what depletes us most, and our permission to recover.

2. GO INTO HIDING

My gym has no mirrors, and it's one of my favorite parts about working out there. It's impossible to stare at your perceived imperfections without a reflective surface, and in my opinion, that leads to a way better workout and overall experience. In many videoconferencing platforms, we are met with our own image in every virtual conversation. It's problematic for two reasons: First, we become more focused on ourselves than others, and second, it can negatively affect how we present ourselves.

How many times have you found yourself checking your image out on a video call? What percentage of the time do you think that you are eye gazing versus paying attention to the speaker? I guarantee the answer to both is "a lot," because we all do it. Sure, you're delightful to look at, and in a sea of possibly unfamiliar faces, yours may feel the most appealing. However, we are gaining little by concentrating on our own image. If we are all focused on ourselves, we're eliminating the point of being on video with other people! It's extremely difficult to connect with others when we aren't even fully paying attention to them. Remember, presence is a core concept of relatability, and our self-focus is an unnecessary distraction.

Second, having self-view enabled can adversely impact not only what you say but how you feel about yourself. Studies have shown that being able to see ourselves during a video chat can make us self-conscious and uncertain and particularly focused on how others perceive us.[2] Confidence and authenticity is a key element of being relat*able* and seeing ourselves on camera can interfere with both.

We aren't exposed to a continuous reflection of ourselves during in-person conversations, so why should we virtually?

Go into hiding. Turn off self-view when you can. If the program you are using doesn't include that option, send them this chapter. (Kidding–kind of.) Or use a sticky note to block your own face. It's an act of self-love and will result in a drastic improvement in your online interactions.

3. CHECK YOURSELF

Yes, I want you to ignore yourself, but not before you check out how you appear in that little window first. Bad video frames are the bathroom selfies of our post-Covid world. You would pay attention to how you presented yourself if you were in person, right? So why are people showing up half-dressed, lying in their unmade bed?

Whether you are connecting virtually for business or pleasure, the experience will result in better connections if you follow these dos and don'ts:

DO:

- **INVEST IN A GOOD CAMERA.** If your built-in camera leaves you fuzzy and glitchy, it's time to upgrade. There are decent webcams that won't break the bank and will show you in a much better light.
- **POSITION THE CAMERA.** I've seen up people's noses. I've seen their feet. I've spent considerable time wondering if I could

count the hairs on an attendee's head. I want to see a shot that catches you from your mid-torso up.

- **DRESS WELL.** At least from the waist up! I love my hoodies, but my super soft "Snuggle Monster" sweatshirt doesn't scream professional. Even though you are home, you can look professional with minimal effort. Put on a real shirt. Make sure it doesn't have massive wrinkles. Frankly, it doesn't even have to be clean; we can't smell you. A little effort goes a long way, and you can still wear your fluffy slippers.

DON'T:

- **FORGET YOUR BACKGROUND.** I can't believe I have to say this, but you shouldn't be Zooming from bed on professional calls. Unless you are catching up with your aunt Patty in Michigan or your BFF in California, give some thought to what people can see behind you. Ask yourself, would I be okay if the world saw this? I'm not a fan of virtual backgrounds, but they do exist for emergency situations. However, "I didn't have time to clean" is not an emergency.
- **SIT IN THE DARK.** We want to see your face, not your shadow. Ring lights are a great add-on, but even simply turning a few lights on in the room makes a difference.

Our image matters, and virtually we only have a small portion of ourselves that we can present. It's important to make the most of it.

UNMASK YOUR EMOTIONS

Masks, while potentially lifesaving, can interfere with our relationship building. In blocking the bottom half of our faces, we reduce the ability to gauge the true emotions of those we connect with. A smile could be completely hidden as our mouths are covered, but a frown emphasized as the brow is front and center. Maybe it's time we all got Botox?

Our brains subconsciously interpret the meaning of facial expressions with surprising accuracy.[3] We read lips without realizing it and naturally assess the movement of each other's mouths, cheeks, eyes, and brow to decipher meaning. When masked, it's easy to see sadness or fear, but more difficult to notice happiness or disgust. The eyes are the windows to the soul, but our whole face is a window to our emotions.

Masks also affect our ability to be empathetic. We subconsciously mimic one another's expressions in conversation without even realizing it.[4] We tend to smile when someone smiles at us. We often frown when they frown. We express sadness when they cry. We cannot mirror what we cannot see, and this can lead to a feeling of disconnection. Think of how you felt the last time someone didn't return your smile. Kind of a bummer, right?

So, what do we do? If we hurt our right leg, our left leg overcompensates to try to mitigate the situation. Similarly, we need to overcompensate the loss of expression with other expressions, specifically our gestures and our words.

You may have previously exchanged a lazy grin with a neighbor, but now your smile has to reach your eyes. Thank you, Tyra, for coining the smize, which is actually backed by science! We as humans are capable of differentiating between smiles with happy eyes, and those with eyes that reveal anger, fear, sadness, or neutrality.[5] We may have been able to display our pursed lips in contemplating a decision, but that may need a furrow of the brow now.

Our overall body language can shift to show more emotion as well. We can move our hands in ways that show our excitement or our opinions ("yeah!" looks different than "no") and gesticulate a bit more energetically than usual. Experts often suggest staying within a boxed area about three feet wide and two feet high surrounding your upper body (lower waist to shoulders). Anything beyond that may look weird, and we're trying to fix weird here.

The most essential aspect of unmasking your emotions is being aware of what may not be visible. It's not necessary to go over the top; a little bit of extra effort goes a long way to get your point, er, emotion across.

FROM A DISTANCE

During quarantine we all essentially ended up in a long-distance relationship . . . with everyone in our lives. Families, friends, loved ones, and colleagues were all kept apart and in some cases remain separated. Staying connected from a distance can require a bit more intentionality than when we see someone in person on a regular basis. Here are four ways you can keep any long-distance relationship alive, from your co-worker to your grandmother:

- **COMMUNICATE.** A lot. Reach out regularly and have conversations that matter. We can maintain a less significant relationship with a random text here and there, but a real connection requires extra attention. Jump on a call, set up a time to be face-to-face virtually, and text regularly to let them know you care. Put in the work.
- **MANAGE EXPECTATIONS.** This is the root of every frustration, and if you and your long-distance counterpart aren't on the same page, someone may feel neglected. How often will you connect? How will you connect? Will you meet up in person at some point?
- **STAY HONEST.** Is something not working? Do you need more or less of something? Staying honest and open when in a remote situation is essential. It's easy to get the vibe that something is "off" when you're often face-to-face but far more difficult to perceive from afar. Express yourself and encourage the expression of others.
- **DO THINGS TOGETHER BUT SEPARATELY.** There are some truly creative ways that you can do activities together even when you're apart. Take a cooking class, learn to mix a new drink, host a trivia night, or watch a movie. The ideas are endless, but the point is the same: Sharing in an experience is a bonding moment.

Each of these tips could apply to any situation, personal or professional. Especially with many workplaces remaining remote, staying connected as a team is essential.

THE LAST WORD . . .

The only constant is change. How things are now may not be the same in a year or five years, but taking a page out of Chapter Seven, it's time to flex our adaptability. We can be virtual rock stars, show our emotions even when half-covered, and stay connected no matter how far. We can do this, because we know that relationships are worth the extra effort.

LET'S DO THIS!

ACTION:

What changes do you commit to making to your video presence?

_____

_____

_____

How can you show your emotions more even when masked?

_____

_____

_____

Are there any long-distance situations in need of your attention?

_____

_____

_____

MINDSET: Relationships are worth the extra effort.

Chapter Fourteen

THE LAST (LAST) WORD

My first trip to Los Angeles remains a lucid memory, as negative experiences often do.

I was traveling to LA to run a booth at a trade show for my company, and I was super excited to check out the west coast. I'm a beach girl, and I was under the impression that Cali would have a few of those. I landed at LAX during a massive heat wave and in the midst of rush hour. I found my transportation and settled in for the seventeen-mile drive from the airport to the convention center downtown, thinking, *I'll be there in thirty minutes max, how bad could it be?* An hour and a half later, and I was still on Interstate 10. I thought there must have been an accident, but no, it was simply regular commuter traffic. I was questioning everyone who had been raving "west coast, best coast."

I finally arrived at the hotel adjacent to the convention center and was excited to be out of a car, train, or plane for a moment. As I entered the lobby, I realized that another hour on the freeway might have been preferable. The beyond-dilapidated interior of the lobby made me terrified to see the condition of my room. As I turned the handle to my "deluxe accommodations" I was assaulted with a foul odor that alluded to stories I never wanted to hear. Online booking fail.

Of course, there were palm trees and sunshine, not that I saw much of either. The only palm trees I encountered were surrounded by cement sidewalks on the walk from the hotel from hell to the fluorescent lights of the convention center. I hated it. I hated everything about LA. I realized how much I disliked Cali when I was happy to be home in New Jersey four days later. I had no desire to return, but I did just that a short time later for another work event.

But that time it was different.

I stayed closer to the ocean and met a guy. Isn't there always a guy?

He was a surfer entrepreneur (how classically LA?!) who lived in Brentwood and asked me to take a walk on the beach. I ended up falling in love because of that sandy stroll. He showed me parts of LA that I never knew existed. We explored everything from the beautiful beaches of Malibu to roadside fish markets to gorgeous hikes where the mountains met the sea. I learned that while there is never a great time to be on the 405, there were times you could avoid it to make it less painful.

When I was asked to host a show based in LA that would require me to move there for six weeks, I jumped at the chance. I embraced the California lifestyle that values self-care and health. I cherished the sunsets, and I never wanted to leave. I was absolutely smitten. Hundred percent in love.

Not with him. With Los Angeles.

There are so many times we don't initially love places or people. Sometimes we have to get to know them a bit better in order to see their potential.

We all have an LA in our lives. There are times we may be an LA in the lives of others.

We might be *this* close, but we're missing so much because we're not looking in the right places. Or having the right conversations. We might be minutes away from a changed life if we find the courage to reach out and say hi even when we don't feel like it.

rela*table* gives us the power to take that next step. To connect with people we may not have initially felt drawn to. To turn our LAs into a lifetime connection. To be an LA in someone else's life by showing them who you are.

I recently caught up with our Chapter One protagonist, Vaughn, who was nearly shaking with all he had to share. "We've been together for eight months, I think she's the one," he said beaming over his beer. "Slow down, Romeo! There's no rush, but tell me about her," I replied. Vaughn filled me in on all the changes since we had last worked together, including his blossoming love life. "It's not always easy. Sometimes I feel like I'm backsliding. I got a promotion recently and now have to be a part of weekly meetings. There are some really smart people in my company, and I worry that I'll sound dumb if I speak up." I asked him what he did when he felt those familiar feelings arise. "I go back to the basics," Vaughn replied. "I remember the steps we went through and remind myself that I'm in my position at work for a reason. I have good ideas and I'm capable of expressing them—even in a room full of people I admire." I hope it doesn't sound patronizing, but I couldn't be prouder.

Becoming relat*able* isn't always linear; like my weight, there are ups and downs. My weight may fluctuate because I ate too many cookies (without regret), but our relatability can waver unexpectedly. Someone says something unkind. We experience a stressful breakup, move, or loss. We don't get enough sleep. We're placed far outside of our comfort zone by something good, like Vaughn's promotion. Whatever the reason for a regression, there is always a remedy. We need to remember to go back to the basics and focus on the cornerstones of relat*able*:

> ***Connect:*** Realize how amazing you are and share yourself with the world. You have so much to offer. Your confidence, positivity, and authenticity will create connections that matter.

> ***Communicate:*** Give yourself the space to adapt to one another and treat people the way they need to be treated, in the moment and in their lives. Know that your presence is always the greatest gift you can give.

> ***Inspire:*** Share your light and your purpose. Finding the spark that ignites it all will change everything.

There may have been someone who made you feel like the center of the universe. Someone who was so real, so true, so authentic that your world changed. That is the power *you* have. You can be that person to someone else. You can change the world by being relat*able*.

LET'S DO THIS!

ACTION:

How will you be more relatable in your interactions?

_____

_____

_____

What's your plan for the times when insecurities pop up?

_____

_____

_____

MINDSET: Nope. No more mindset prompts; it's time to *do*. It's time to take action. It's time to implement everything you have learned, all of the shifts, and get out there and be relatable. I can't wait to hear all about it.

ACKNOWLEDGMENTS

Writing a book is both a solitary and collaborative experience. Many hours, days, and months were spent between just me and my laptop, but those moments aren't what truly created the book that you are reading right now and are continuing to read through these love notes to all who made this happen! Thank you!

First and foremost, I'd like to thank the love of my life, Kevin. Our kitchen conversations led to the development of relat*able* as a concept and "big idea" years ago. Your endless support and encouragement reminded me that this book needed to be in the world, and that I was the person to write it. You are my best friend, soul mate, and an incredible writer with brilliant ideas. Everyone needs a Kevin. Well, not my Kevin.

After the idea came to fruition, it landed in the hands of my capable friend, editor, and writer Jen Singer. Thank you for seeing relat*able*'s potential from the start and helping me shape the idea into a proposal that a publisher would fall in love with. Thank you to my amazing agent, Amanda Luedeke, for taking that proposal and placing it in the perfect publisher's proverbial hands.

Tiller Press, thank you for believing in the power of relat*able*. To my editor, Ronnie Alvarado, thank you for helping to ensure it all made sense and the book never lost my tone, for better or worse. It almost felt too easy to work together, but in my experience, that's a sign of an amazing relationship.

Finally, thank you to my family. To my parents, who have been my most steadfast supporters since birth. Thank you for giving me the space to grow, the love to feel safe during the most challenging times, and a soft place to land when I needed it. To my children, who are stuck with me forever, I love you more than I could ever express. Everything I do, I do for you.

Wait, one more! Thank you to *you*, dear reader. I appreciate you. Thank you for spending your time with me and allowing me to take up precious space in your head. I don't take that for granted. I'm forever grateful to you.

NOTES

CHAPTER ONE: FAR FROM ALONE

1. Patricia Greenfield, "Social Change, Cultural Evolution, and Human Development," *Current Opinion in Psychology* 8 (2016): 84-92, doi:10.1016 /j.copsyc.2015.10.012.
2. Jonathan Chew, "Why Most Millennials Find Holiday Gatherings Stressful," December 22, 2015, https://fortune.com/2015/12/22/social-anxiety-joyable/.
3. Alisa Hrustic, "Young People Don't Know How to Talk to Each Other Anymore," February 25, 2019, https://www.menshealth.com/trending-news/a19544562 /millennials-awkward-conversations/.
4. Ibid.
5. Jamie Ballard, "Millennials Are the Loneliest Generation," July 30, 2019, https://today.yougov.com/topics/lifestyle/articles-reports/2019/07/30 /loneliness-friendship-new-friends-poll-survey?subId1=xid:fr1583966251 230hfb.
6. Ibid.
7. Smith Holt-Lunstad, "Loneliness and Social Isolation as Risk Factors for Mortality: A Meta-Analytic Review," *Perspectives on Psychological Science* 10, no. 2 (2015): 227-37.
8. Christian Hakulinen et al., "Correction: Social Isolation and Loneliness as Risk Factors for Myocardial Infarction, Stroke and Mortality: UK Biobank Cohort Study of 479 054 Men and Women," *Heart* 105, no. 14 (2019), https://doi .org/10.1136/heartjnl-2017-312663corr1.
9. Day Mallen, "Online Versus Face-to-Face Conversation: An Examination of Relational and Discourse Variables," *Psychotherapy* 40, nos. 1-2 (2003): 155-63.
10. Bradley M. Okdie et al., "Getting to Know You: Face-to-Face Versus Online Interactions," *PsycEXTRA Dataset*, 2010, https://doi.org/10.1037/e566842012 -162.

CHAPTER TWO: WHY PEOPLE LIKE PEOPLE

1. "UMass Amherst Researcher Finds Most People Lie in Everyday Conversation," June 10, 2002, https://www.umass.edu/newsoffice/article/umass -amherst-researcher-finds-most-people-lie-everyday-conversation.
2. Michelle Drouin et al., "Why Do People Lie Online? 'Because Everyone Lies on the Internet,'" *Computers in Human Behavior* 64 (2016): 134-42, https://doi .org/10.1016/j.chb.2016.06.052.
3. Matt Blanchard and Barry A. Farber, "Lying in Psychotherapy: Why and What Clients Don't Tell Their Therapist about Therapy and Their Relationship," *Disclosure and Concealment in Psychotherapy*, November 2018, pp. 90-112, https://doi.org/10.4324/9781315229034-6.

4. Susan Guibert, "Study: Telling Fewer Lies Linked to Better Health and Relationships," Phys.org, August 6, 2012, https://phys.org/news/2012-08-lies-linked-health-relationships.html.

5. Travis Bradberry, "10 Things You Do That Make You Less Likable," July 1, 2016, https://www.businessinsider.com/10-things-you-do-that-make-you-less-likable-2016-6.

6. Liz Mineo, "Over Nearly 80 Years, Harvard Study Has Been Showing How to Live a Healthy and Happy Life," November 26, 2018, https://news.harvard.edu/gazette/story/2017/04/over-nearly-80-years-harvard-study-has-been-showing-how-to-live-a-healthy-and-happy-life/.

7. Tanya Ghahremani, "The Worst People in Reality TV History," August 14, 2013, https://www.complex.com/pop-culture/2013/08/worst-reality-tv-stars-ever/.

CHAPTER THREE: CONNECT— AUTHENTICALLY YOU

1. Thomas Curran, "Is Perfectionism Rising over Time? A Meta-Analysis of Birth Cohort Differences from 1989 to 2016," 2018, https://doi.org/10.31234/osf.io/pkvxa.

2. Ibid.

3. Michelle Drouin et al., "Why Do People Lie Online? 'Because Everyone Lies on the Internet,'" *Computers in Human Behavior* 64 (2016): 134-42, https://doi.org/10.1016/j.chb.2016.06.052.

4. Bella DePaulo et al., "Lying in Everyday Life," *Journal of Personality and Social Psychology* 70, no. 5 (May 1996): 979-95.

5. "Lying Less Linked to Better Health, New Research Finds," American Psychological Association, https://www.apa.org/news/press/releases/2012/08/lying-less.

6. Patrick Krill et al., "The Prevalence of Substance Use and Other Mental Health Concerns Among American Attorneys," *Journal of Addiction Medicine* 10, no. 1 (2016): 46-52, https://doi.org/10.1097/adm.0000000000000182

CHAPTER FOUR: CONNECT— CONFIDENCE FOR DAYS

1. William James, *Psychology: The Briefer Course* (Mineola, NY: Dover, 2017).

2. Norman Goodman and Stanley Coopersmith, "The Antecedents of Self-Esteem," *American Sociological Review* 34, no. 1 (1969): 116, https://doi.org/10.2307/2092806.

3. John P. Robinson, Phillip R. Shaver, and Lawrence S. Wrightsman, *Measures of Personality and Social Psychological Attitudes: Measures of Social Psychological Attitudes* (St. Louis: Elsevier Science, 2014).

4. Crista A. Brett, Alan S. Brett, and Sarah S. Shaw, "Impact of Traumatic Incidents on Family-of-Origin Functioning: An Empirical Study," *Journal of Contemporary Psychotherapy* 23, no. 4 (1993): 255-66, https://doi.org/10.1007/bf00946086.

5. Paul R. Amato, Laura Spencer Loomis, and Alan Booth, "Parental Divorce, Marital Conflict, and Offspring Well-Being during Early Adulthood," *Social Forces* 73, no. 3 (1995): 895, https://doi.org/10.2307/2580551.

6. Dana R. Carney, Amy J.C. Cuddy, and Andy J. Yap, "Power Posing," *Psychological Science* 21, no. 10 (2010): 1363-68, https://doi .org/10.1177/0956797610383437.

7. Lawrence A. Hosman and Susan A. Siltanen, "Powerful and Powerless Language Forms," *Journal of Language and Social Psychology* 25, no. 1 (2006): 33-46, https://doi.org/10.1177/0261927x05284477.

8. Paula Niedenthal et al., "Embodiment in Attitudes, Social Perception, and Emotion," *Personality and Social Psychology Review* 9, no. 3 (2016): 184-211.

CHAPTER FIVE: CONNECT—
POWER OF POSITIVITY

1. Antonio Zuffianò et al., "The Positivity Scale: Concurrent and Factorial Validity Across Late Childhood and Early Adolescence," *Frontiers in Psychology* 10 (2019), https://doi.org/10.3389/fpsyg.2019.00831.

2. Eric Kim et al., "Optimism and Cause-Specific Mortality: A Prospective Cohort Study," *American Journal of Epidemiology* 185, no. 1 (2017): 21-29, doi:10.1093 /aje/kww182.

3. Lisa Yanek et al., "Effect of Positive Well-Being on Incidence of Symptomatic Coronary Artery Disease," *American Journal of Cardiology* 112, no. 8 (October 2013): 1120-25.

4. Julia Boehm and Sonja Lyubomirsky, "Does Happiness Promote Career Success?," *Journal of Career Assessment* 16, no. 1 (February 2008): 101-16, doi:10.1177/1069072707308140.

5. Marian Kohut et al., "Exercise and Psychosocial Factors Modulate Immunity to Influenza Vaccine in Elderly Individuals," *Journals of Gerontology Series A: Biological Sciences and Medical Sciences* 57, no. 9 (2002), doi:10.1093 /gerona/57.9.m557.

6. "How Deadly Is Quicksand?," *Encyclopaedia Britannica*, https://www .britannica.com/story/how-deadly-is-quicksand.

7. Joyce Shaffer, "Neuroplasticity and Positive Psychology in Clinical Practice: A Review for Combined Benefits," *Psychology* 3, no. 12 (2012): 1110-15, doi:10.4236/psych.2012.312a164.

8. Jean Knox, "The Mindful Brain: Reflection and Attunement in the Cultivation of Wellbeing by Siegel, Daniel J," *Journal of Analytical Psychology* 54, no. 2 (2009): 284-85.

9. Daniel Nettle, *Happiness: The Science Behind Your Smile* (Oxford: Oxford University Press, 2005).

10. Gian Vittorio Caprara et al., "Positive Orientation: Explorations on What Is Common to Life Satisfaction, Self-Esteem, and Optimism," *Epidemiologia e Psichiatria Sociale* 19, no. 1 (2010): 63-71, https://doi.org/10.1017 /s1121189x00001615.

11. Bernadette P. Luengo Kanacri et al., "Longitudinal Relations Among Positivity,

Perceived Positive School Climate, and Prosocial Behavior in Colombian Adolescents," *Child Development* 88, no. 4 (2017): 1100-14, https://doi.org/10.1111/cdev.12863.

12. Antonio Zuffianò et al., "The Positivity Scale: Concurrent and Factorial Validity Across Late Childhood and Early Adolescence," *Frontiers in Psychology* 10 (2019), https://doi.org/10.3389/fpsyg.2019.00831.

13. Chris Weller, "A Neuroscientist Who Studies Decision-Making Reveals the Most Important Choice You Can Make," *Business Insider*, July 28, 2017, https://www.businessinsider.com/neuroscientist-most-important-choice-in-life-2017-7.

14. Julie Tseng and Jordan Poppenk, "Brain Meta-State Transitions Demarcate Thoughts across Task Contexts, Exposing the Mental Noise of Trait Neuroticism," 2019, https://doi.org/10.1101/576298.

15. Richard Weaver et al., "Destructive Dialogue: Negative Self-Talk and Positive Imaging," *College Student Journal* 22, no. 3 (1988): 230-40; Susan G. Ziegler, "Negative Thought Stopping," *Journal of Physical Education, Recreation & Dance* 58, no. 4 (1987): 66-69, https://doi.org/10.1080/07303084.1987.10603869.

16. Jacqueline Fagard, "Early Development of Hand Preference and Language Lateralization: Are They Linked, and If So, How?," *Developmental Psychobiology* 55, no. 6 (2013): 596-607, https://doi.org/10.1002/dev.21131; Eileen Luders et al., "The Unique Brain Anatomy of Meditation Practitioners: Alterations in Cortical Gyrification," *Frontiers in Human Neuroscience* 6 (2012), https://doi.org/10.3389/fnhum.2012.00034.

CHAPTER SIX: COMMUNICATE— PRESENCE OVER PRESENTS

1. Maxwell King, *The Good Neighbor: The Life and Work of Fred Rogers* (Farmington Hills, MI: Large Print Press, 2019).

2. Chris L. Kleinke, "Gaze and Eye Contact: A Research Review," *Psychological Bulletin* 100, no. 1 (1986): 78-100, https://doi.org/10.1037/0033-2909.100.1.78.

3. Teresa Farroni et al., "Eye Contact Detection in Humans from Birth," *Proceedings of the National Academy of Sciences* 99, no. 14 (2002): 9602-05, doi:10.1073/pnas.152159999.

4. Ibid.

5. Shogo Kajimura and Michio Nomura, "When We Cannot Speak: Eye Contact Disrupts Resources Available to Cognitive Control Processes during Verb Generation," *Cognition* 157 (2016): 352-57, https://doi.org/10.1016/j.cognition.2016.10.002.

6. Nicola Binetti et al., "Pupil Dilation as an Index of Preferred Mutual Gaze Duration," *Royal Society Open Science* 3, no. 7 (2016): 160086, https://doi.org/10.1098/rsos.160086.

7. Jamie Ducharme, "What Is Phubbing? Why It's Bad for Relationships and Mental Health," *Time*, March 29, 2018, https://time.com/5216853/what-is-phubbing/.

8. Varoth Chotpitayasunondh and Karen M. Douglas, "The Effects of 'Phubbing'

on Social Interaction," *Journal of Applied Social Psychology* 48 (2018): 304-16, https://doi.org/10.1111/jasp.12506.

9. Vahid Kohpeima Jahromi et al., "Active Listening: The Key of Successful Communication in Hospital Managers," *Electronic Physician* 8, no. 3 (2016): 2123-28, https://doi.org/10.19082/2123.

CHAPTER TWELVE: THE CRITICAL SMILE

1. John Gottman, *What Predicts Divorce: The Relationship between Marital Processes & Marital Outcomes* (New York: Lawrence Earlbaum, 1994).

2. Marcial Losada and Emily Heaphy. "The Role of Positivity and Connectivity in the Performance of Business Teams: A Nonlinear Dynamics Model," *American Behavioral Scientist* 47, no. 6 (February 2004): 740-65, https://doi.org/10.1177/0002764203260208.

3. Barbara L. Fredrickson, "Updated Thinking on Positivity Ratios," *American Psychologist* 68, no. 9 (December 2013): 814-22.

CHAPTER THIRTEEN: SMIZING IS REAL

1. Carlos Ferran and Stephanie Watts, "Videoconferencing in the Field: A Heuristic Processing Model," *Management Science* 54, no. 9 (September 1, 2008): 1565-78.

2. Matthew K. Miller, Regan L. Mandryk, Max V. Birk, Ansgar E. Depping, and Tushita Patel, "Through the Looking Glass," *Proceedings of the 2017 CHI Conference on Human Factors in Computing Systems*, 2017, https://doi.org/10.1145/3025453.3025548.

3. Chris Frith, "Role of Facial Expressions in Social Interactions," *Philosophical Transactions: Biological Sciences* 364, no. 1535 (December 12, 2009): 3453-58.

4. Martin Wegrzyn, Maria Vogt, Berna Kireclioglu, Julia Schneider, and Johanna Kissler, "Mapping the Emotional Face: How Individual Face Parts Contribute to Successful Emotion Recognition," *PLoS One* 12, no. 5 (2017), https://doi.org/10.1371/journal.pone.0177239.

5. Mario Del Líbano, Manuel G. Calvo, Andrés Fernández-Martín, and Guillermo Recio, "Discrimination between Smiling Faces: Human Observers vs. Automated Face Analysis," *Acta Psychologica* 187 (2018): 19-29, https://doi.org/10.1016/j.actpsy.2018.04.019.

ABOUT THE AUTHOR

Rachel DeAlto is a relationship expert, media personality, and keynote speaker. Rachel has appeared as an expert on Lifetime's *Married at First Sight* and TLC's *Kate+Date* and is presently engaged as Match's Chief Dating Expert. Rachel maintains a law degree from Seton Hall University, a masters in psychology from Arizona State University, and an undergraduate degree in communications from Syracuse University. Rachel is a regular contributor on TV news programs and talk shows, including *Good Morning America*, *Tamron Hall*, *Access Hollywood*, *CNN*, and *Today*. She has also given three TEDx talks including "Being Authentic in a Filtered World," which is featured on TED.com. Rachel lives in New Jersey with her family, where she enjoys laughing at her own jokes and playing with her dog, Mac.